2/20/98

Timothy Adams Jr.

Also by the author

The Myth of Black Capitalism
Let Your Motto Be Resistance
The Mugging of Black America
Black Fatherhood: The Guide to Male Parenting
Black Fatherhood II: Black Women Talk about Their Men
Blacks and Reds: Race and Class in Conflict, 1919–1990
Betrayed: The History of Presidential Failure to Protect
   Black Lives
Beyond O.J.: Race, Sex and Class Lessons for America

The Assassination

of the Black Male Image

Earl Ofari Hutchinson, Ph.D.

A TOUCHSTONE BOOK
Published by Simon & Schuster

TOUCHSTONE
Rockefeller Center
1230 Avenue of the Americas
New York, NY 10020

Copyright © 1994, 1996 by Earl Ofari Hutchinson, Ph.D.
All rights reserved,
including the right of reproduction
in whole or in part in any form.

First Touchstone Edition 1997

TOUCHSTONE and colophon are registered trademarks
of Simon & Schuster Inc.

Designed by Deirdre C. Amthor

Manufactured in the United States of America

10   9   8   7   6   5   4   3   2   1

Library of Congress Cataloging-in-Publication Data is available.

ISBN 0-684-83100-7
    0-684-83657-2 (pbk)

Acknowledgments

Special thanks to Matt Blair, Rene Childress, Jim Hornfischer, and, of course, my wife BBH for bouncing my sometimes crooked ideas back to me on a straight line.

Contents

Aunt Sally: "What's kep' you—boat get aground?"

Huck: "Yes'm—she—"

Aunt Sally: "Don't say yes'm—say Aunt Sally. Where'd she get aground?"

Huck: I didn't know what to say because I didn't know whether the boat would be coming up the river or down. Now I struck an idea, and fetched it out: "It warn't the grounding—that didn't keep us back but a little. We blowed out a cylinder head."

Aunt Sally: "Good gracious! anybody hurt?"

Huck: "No'm killed a nigger."

Aunt Sally: "Well, it's lucky; because sometimes people do get hurt."

Mark Twain, *The Adventures of Huckleberry Finn,* Chapter 17

The Growth Industry in Black Male Mythology: An Overview

I did not applaud Bill Clinton's "racial healing" speech delivered at the University of Texas, Austin, in October 1995 after the Million Man March on Washington and the O. J. Simpson acquittal. He asked blacks to understand white fears about crime, drugs, and welfare. Why? Those fears are based on ancient, decrepit, and for the most part discredited myths and stereotypes. But well-meaning Willie was undaunted; he confidently repeated the worst of them.[1]

The perennial favorite stereotype Clinton repeated: "Violence for white people too often comes with a black face."

Like everyone else Willie knows that two men face trial in the bombing of the Oklahoma City federal building in April 1995. It was the worst mass-murder terror attack in American history. Their faces are white, not black. But Willie was right. Many whites get cold, chilling nightmares about being attacked by blacks even though their waking reality is that their attacker will almost always be white. The majority of violent crime against whites are committed by other whites, and in most cases not on media-dubbed "crime-scarred" ghetto streets but out in pristine suburbia.

It's true that in 1994 blacks committed nearly half of the murders and robberies—according to official arrest and report figures, anyway—and nearly all of their victims were other blacks. Once again we have figures proving, if proof is needed, that blacks are a menace not to society but to themselves.[2]

The most popular stereotype Clinton repeated:

"It isn't racist for whites to say they don't understand why people put up with . . . drugs being sold in the schools or in the open."

Willie and anyone else who believes that should check out the annual University of Michigan study which more than confirms that the overwhelming majority of drug users, abusers, and sellers in America are white. Drug peddling is rampant on the campuses, in bars, at rock concerts, and at other suburban hot spots. It's gotten so bad that a few more stray reports and features are slowly inching their way into the media about the sons and daughters of suburbia using, abusing, dealing, and OD'ing on drugs. Neither I, nor anyone else, should take delight in the fact that more whites are menaces to society, too, but it's something that must be said. I'll have more to say on this later.[3]

This is the stereotype Clinton repeated that politicians, much of the media, and the experts who have turned studying black deviancy into a growth industry love to spout:

"It's not racist for whites to assert that the culture of welfare dependency . . . cannot be broken . . . unless there is first more personal responsibility."

Let's keep this one simple. More than two out of three welfare recipients are white. There are just as many daddies missing from white homes as from black homes. I'll have much more to say about this later, too.[4]

If Willie the racial healer really believed one or more of the stereotypes that black men are criminals, derelict, lazy, violence-prone, and sexually irresponsible dregs, I wouldn't be surprised.

The image of the malevolent black male is based on a durable and time-resistant bedrock of myths, half-truths, and lies. The image was created during the European conquest of Africa, nurtured during slavery, artfully refined during the nadir of segregation, and revived during the Ronald Reagan–George Bush–Newt Gingrich years. I'm not picking only on Willie. Many have profited handsomely from the lucrative growth industry America has fashioned out of black-male bashing.

To maintain power and control, the plantation masters said that black men were savage and hypersexual. To strengthen racial control, late nineteenth- and early-twentieth-century scientists and academics concocted pseudo-theories that said black men were criminal and mentally defective. To justify lynching and political domination, the politicians and business leaders of the era said that black men were rapists and brutes. To roll back civil rights and slash social programs, Reagan–Rush Limbaugh–Pat Buchanan–type conservatives say black men are derelict and lazy. That's only one side of the race hustle coin. There's another even more insidious, disgusting, and dangerous side to that coin.[5]

To secure big Hollywood contracts and media stardom, some young black filmmakers say the "boyz N the hood" are gangbangers, drive-by shooters, dope dealers, and carjackers. To hustle mega record deals and concert bookings, some rappers and comedians say black men are "niggers" and, more incredibly, "bitches." To nail down book contracts and TV talk show appearances, some black feminist writers say black men are sexist exploiters or, put less charitably, "dogs."

The corporate-controlled media defiantly drops the words "racism" and "economic injustice" from its vocabulary. It pounds, twists, and slants all of these stereotypes into sensational headlines, sound bites, and doctored photos, and dumps them back on the public as fact.

A black man can be wealthy, possess status, be politically and socially connected, and still wind up on the image assassin's list. The glitter and glamour of the entertainment world couldn't save Michael Jackson or Spike Lee. The fan adulation and megacontracts in the sports world couldn't save Michael Jordan or Mike Tyson. The rarefied atmosphere of politics couldn't save Adam Clayton Powell or Clarence Thomas. The social activism of the black freedom movement couldn't save Martin Luther King, Malcolm X, Marcus Garvey, Paul Robeson, or W. E. B. Du Bois.

III

What about black women? Aren't they victims, too? Of course, many black women are poor, raped, battered, abused, called "bitches" and "hos," and stuck with bills and babies. Some black men do these things to black women.

But America has not made the black woman its universal bogeyman. The black man is. Here are four reasons why I say that. First, I'm a black man. I hear, see, and feel the pain of black men daily. Second, I can count. For a black man, here's the grim picture: He will live, on average, to be sixty-seven years old. She will live to be seventy-three years old. He's one and one-half times more likely than she is to drop dead of a heart attack. He will have a far greater death rate from cancer, stroke, pneumonia, or AIDS.[6]

Then there are the unnatural causes of death. Compared to her, he's five times more likely to kill himself by his own hand, three times more likely to be killed in a car accident, and four times more likely to be killed by someone else. Meanwhile, one out of three young black males languish in prison, on parole, or on probation. One out of seven will be murdered. One out of three black males is unemployed.[7]

Third, I know another one of America's dirty little secrets. Many Americans hate and fear black men. Yet they are fascinated with them. They love to see them sing, dance, lug, and toss those balls. In deeply sexist America, the game is still about white male ego, power, and control. Black men are perceived as threats to all.

Fourth, black women are black and poorer. They drag around their own trunk jampacked with racist stereotypes. They have been branded as mammies, sapphires, sexpots, welfare queens, baby makers, deadbeats, golddiggers, and increasingly as more crime- and violence-prone. They are fast becoming the other menace to society. Yet black women, like all women in a male-dominated society, are also shoved to the political and economic outer limits.

Note: Hillary could tell Willie something about stereotypes. The Republicans had a field day crucifying and demonizing her for Whitewater. Why not? She was a Democrat, the President's wife, and a woman. This made her triply vulnerable. If nothing else, the way she was treated by the public and much of the press should have given Willie some insight into the bitter truth: stereotypes take no prisoners even when the victim's name is Clinton.

But the privileged and wealthy men that call the shots in America don't need to wage the same ego war against black women as they do against black men. They occasionally depict her as a woman always burdened and eternally suffering. They tell her that she wouldn't be in the mess she's in if *he* would just get a job, stay out of jail, stop shooting or snorting up, get married or stop making babies and quit dropping dead so fast (for some not fast enough).

The plot to assassinate the black male image has deep roots in America's sinister racial past. To understand the complexity of the plot and the circle of conspirators, we'll start with the era when many white Americans dropped the code words, skipped the niceties, and called the black man what they truly thought he was: a beast.

Chapter 1

The Negro: A Beast . . . or in the Image of God?

I wish Rodney King had read Charles Carroll's *The Negro a Beast or in the Image of God*. He might understand why many people said rotten things about him. This is what I mean. In November 1992, King spoke to about seventy-five students at Tustin High School in the mostly white suburban bedroom community of Orange County. This was King's first major public appearance in nearly a year. King, being a modest, unassuming man, had purposely kept a low profile.[1]

It didn't help. People still bad-mouthed him. They called him a doper, an alcoholic, and a violence-prone ex-convict. Many openly grumbled that King himself had provoked the cops. Some even smirked and whispered that he deserved the ass-whipping. In the Simi Valley trial of the four LAPD cops who beat King, defense attorneys in a bravura performance used this sneaky racism to their advantage and got them off. One unnamed juror said of King, "He was obviously a dangerous person, [with a] massive size and threatening actions."[2]

King, and his attorney, Milton Grimes, were fed up with this kind of talk. They figured that high school students would be sympathetic. King, himself a high school dropout, would benignly tell the kids to stay in school. They hoped this would improve his image.

It didn't. The following day, angry readers deluged the *Los Angeles Times* with calls objecting to school officials letting "a dangerous parolee" on a high school campus. The Tustin High School principal felt the heat, back-pedaled fast, and claimed it was all a mistake. Sounding properly indignant, he agreed that King was not a suitable "role model."[3]

Note: *The hapless King got millions for his troubles in a settlement with the City of Los Angeles. But he was far from out of the woods. In sentencing the two cops who beat King, federal judge Arthur Davies practically pinned a medal on them, and blamed King for getting his butt kicked and starting the riots. In the next five years after the beating he was stopped, arrested, searched, and hassled eight times by police in half a dozen cities. His wife finally said enough is enough and dumped him. Was King shell-shocked, walking comatose, brain-damaged, a natural loser, or simply a black guy who got the raw end of a baton and would forever pay the price?[4]*

II

He was "dangerous," of "massive size," "threatening," and "a poor role model." Remember the words of the King juror as I turn back the pages of history a century and more. Carroll said that and much more about black men in his grotesque little book published in 1900. Reading the passages of his book even without the filter of America's hideous racial past, one might have reason to laugh.

Carroll, however, was dead serious. His book was not published by the Ku Klux Klan in rural Mississippi or Alabama, but by the American Book and Bible House in St. Louis. He spent fifteen years and $20,000 digging in the archives and consulting with theologians, academics, and scientists to get the goods on "the negro beast." The book was a brisk seller. Carroll argued that the black man was left out of human creation and was a subspecies of the animal world.

Carroll was not a quack. He did not make any of this up. He considered himself a man of pure science. He based his "theory" on the meticulous research of Alexander Winchell, a distinguished professor of geology and paleontology at the University of Michigan. When the evidence got a little skimpy in some places, Carroll retreated into Scripture. He swore that God warned that since creation the world's troubles had begun when human beings let the Negro "beast" mingle among them.[5]

Carroll had his critics. Georgia theologian W. S. Armstead was indignant that he would dare bring the word of God into this. By calling black men beasts, he felt Carroll was letting them off the hook. Armstead said the black man was a cunning, calculating degenerate who followed his "murderous heart" and brutally "waylaid" white women.

Armstead didn't have much chance against learned men like Carroll and Winchell. They were Northerners and for nearly a half century they had beaten the South to the punch every time when it came to propagating myths about black bestiality.[6]

George Fitzhugh, a Virginia newspaperman, sometime planter and always articulate defender of slavery was delighted to find that his Northern brethren were very receptive to his views. In 1854, in *Sociology for the South,* Fitzhugh wrote that "slavery rescued blacks from idolatry and cannibalism, and every brutal vice and crime that can disgrace humanity."

Fitzhugh took his act on the road and headed North. He quickly discovered that many influential power brokers thought that his *Sociology for the South* should be the sociology for the North. Many leading newspapermen quoted him. Businessmen wined and dined him. Some Northern congressman snipped quotes from his writings and placed them into the *Congressional Globe* (later *Record*).[7]

During the Civil War, dozens of Northern newspaper editors and politicians were livid because Old Abe and his Republican political cronies had the audacity to shed white blood to free black savages. At every turn, they raised the bloody flag and tried to sabotage the war effort.

Note: Every first-year history student knows that the Founding Fathers railed against slavery while sipping mint juleps their slaves served them and counting the big bucks their bucks/slaves made for them. What first year students don't know is that the wig-wearing Founding Fathers were good mentors for the Carrolls, Fitzhughs, et al. They also propagated the cherished myths, lies, and half-truths about blacks that still pulsate in America today. A sampling:

Washington: "most of them will slight their work, or be idle altogether." (lazy, derelict)

Jefferson: "in reason much inferior [to whites] . . . in imagination . . . dull, tasteless and anomalous." [low to no IQ]

Madison: "Their estates are surrounded by vicious free blacks . . . keep the minds of their owners in a state of perpetual suspicion, fear." [the original menace-to-society utterance]

Adams: "robbery, plunder and massacre to preserve their lives" [His short list of black traits packed all the stereotypes in].[8]

III

The Civil War ended legal slavery, but it did not put the old planters entirely out of business. They still had one big trump card to play: The BIG BLACK SCARE. They played it hard by convincing whites, North and South, that blacks were out to get land, power, and white women. Soon men in white sheets silhouetted the night sky with their fiery crosses. Their terror campaign to whip the black beasts back in line was a smashing success.[9]

Reconstruction was dead. The abolitionists who had pricked the conscience of the nation were too old and tired to care anymore. The ranks of the Radical Republicans in Congress were thinning by the hour. And Northern whites were dead set against risking their necks to fight for the rights of men who they didn't really believe were men anyway.[10]

Meantime, the learned men of the North like Carroll were busy mangling science to shape the image of the black man as criminal, sex-crazed, violent, and degenerate. They deliberately distorted Charles Darwin's race-neutral biological theory of "natural selection" in human evolution to make their case that whites were the superior race and that blacks were genetically inferior and sexually savage. Dr. Frank Hoffman, in 1896, backed Carroll to the hilt. Hoffman, like Carroll, was not a Southerner. In fact, he was not a Northerner. In fact, he was not even an American. Hoffman, writing from Germany, declared that there was such an "immense amount of immorality and crime" among black men it had to be part of their "race traits and tendencies."

The message to worried whites: Sit back, relax, and let nature take its course. All those decadent black men would soon die out from their own "inferior organs and constitutional weaknesses." Hoffman's wise words were rushed into print by the prestigious American Economic Association (AEA).

Another learned Northerner, Walter F. Wilcox, chief statistician for the U.S. Census Bureau, thought the good doctor had the right *Zeitgeist*. Three years later, with the blessing of the American Social Science Association, Wilcox pinned up his charts, juggled figures, and solemnly predicted that blacks were "several times" more likely to commit crime than whites. He wasn't finished. The next year he told the social scientists that Hoffman was right. Blacks were doomed to go the way of the dodo bird and dinosaur because of "disease, vice and profound discouragement."[11]

The American Economic Association was on a fast track to get the official words of its scholars out to the public. They rushed historian Paul Tillinghast's paper "The Negro in Africa and America" into print. Tillinghast agreed with the other scholars. He cautioned them not to forget that blacks were "seriously handicapped by the inherited conditions" they brought with them from savage Africa.

Around the same time, Dr. G. Stanley Hall was determined not to be outdone by the AEA. The president of the American Psychological Association and founder of the *American Journal of Psychology* thought his fellow academics were putting too much emphasis on "race traits." As a clinician, he believed there were murky forces at work in the black psyche. According to his diagnosis, the black man's "disthesis, both psychic and physical is erethic, volatile, changeable, prone to transcoidal, intensely emotional and even epileptoid states." Buried somewhere between the "erethic" and "transcoidal" gibberish was a hopeless dimwit. The public had to be on the alert.[12]

A future President didn't dispute this. In 1901, in the *Atlantic Monthly,* Princeton University professor and native Southerner Woodrow Wilson asked what could one really expect of individuals who were really little more than a "host of dusky children," "insolent and aggressive, sick of work, covetous of pleasure." [13]

The lineup of highbrow intellectual magazines that endorsed this gobbledygook read like a roll call of academia. They included *Popular Science Monthly,* the *Annals of the American Academy of Political and Social Science, Medicine,* and the *North American Review.* They all chimed in with volumes of heady research papers, articles, and scholarly opinions that proved blacks were hopelessly inferior, crime- and violence-prone defectives from which society had to be protected.[14]

The studies by these academics touched off yet another explosion of pseudo-scholarly books by writers during the first decade of the 1900s on black men's alleged bestiality. A choice sampling:

- William P. Calhoun, *The Caucasian and the Negro in the United States* (1902)
- William B. Smith, *The Color Line: A Brief in Behalf of the Unborn* (1905)
- Robert W. Shufeldt, *The Negro, a Menace to American Civilization* (1907)[15]

I threw the last one in just in case you thought that Hollywood was original when it dreamed up the title for the film *Menace to Society.*

Note: *I hate to give these two guys any more attention than they deserve but there's no way around them to make my point effectively that the past never dies.* Bell Curve *author Charles*

Murray scored big with conclusions like this: "A large majority of the next generation of blacks in the inner city are growing up without fathers and with limited cognitive ability."

The other one, End of Racism *author Dinesh D'Souza had none of the academic pretensions of a Murray. By that I mean he didn't load up his phony theories on black intellectual inferiority with pages of graphs, charts, stats, studies, and out-of-context expert quotes. He got right to the point: slavery was essentially benign, segregation was benevolent, and civil rights laws and the evil affirmative action rulings made America a color-blind society. Yet nothing has helped stem "the breakdown of civilization within the African-American community."*

These guys were the talk of the academic and literary world in 1994 and 1995. Their books soared to the top of charts. They were trotted around to every TV talk show imaginable. While the debates over their "theories" raged, they made a mint and laughed all the way to the bank.[16]

IV

Since art does imitate life, it was only a matter of time before this pap crept into the literature. At first, Northern and Southern novelists did not lay it on too thick. The blacks in their stories were mostly grinning, buck-dancing, lazy, slightly larcenous darkies. As the scientists kept up their drumbeat warnings about the black menace, the novelists soon turned vicious. Upton Sinclair had impeccable credentials as a socialist crusader. Still, in his popular muckraking novel *The Jungle,* published in 1906, Sinclair was appalled that white girls working in Chicago's hellish stockyards rubbed shoulders "with big black buck Negroes with daggers in their boots."[17]

This was far too tame for Thomas Nelson Page. He wasn't a man of subtlety when it came to racial matters. But first he had to lay the proper groundwork. In an essay called "The Negro: The Southerner's Problem," he warned that the old-time darkies were dying off and that the "new issue" was "lazy, thriftless, intemperate, insolent, dishonest and without the most rudimentary elements of morality." In his novel *Red Rock,* he continued to warn of the dangers of the black peril.

Even this didn't satisfy Thomas Dixon. Page only talked about the "new issue" Negro. Dixon set out to vanquish him. In his big, sprawling novel *The Clansman,* published in 1905, Dixon described him as "half child, half animal, the sport of impulse, whim and conceit . . . a being who left to his will, roams at night and sleeps in the day, whose speech knows no word of love, whose passions once aroused, are as the fury of the tiger." It sent collective chills up the spines of much of white America. Bolt the doors. Turn out the lights. Praise the Lord and pass the ammunition. The black beast was coming. In *The Clansman,* Dixon had the right men to defend society and (white womanhood) from this creature: the Ku Klux Klan.[18]

Dixon knew he was on to something big. When *The Clansman* was adapted for the stage, it brought down theater houses everywhere. Audiences were delirious. They had to see the KKK destroy the black beasts. Soon Broadway's Great White Way picked up on Dixon and made him the toast of New York. The trendy magazine *Theatre IV* gave him a free platform to explain "Why I Wrote *The Clansman.*" Dixon swore he wasn't a bigot; the book, he said, was based on "historical authenticity." The *New York Evening Post* was impressed. It praised him for tackling "a question of tremendously vital importance."[19]

Filmmaker D. W. Griffith wanted Americans to know just how important it was. Less than a decade later, he turned *The Clansman* into *The Birth of a Nation.* He brushed off vehement protests from the NAACP and black leaders that it was all a lie. He could afford to. By then cash registers were jingling everywhere as the film smashed house records nationally. When the film hit the White House, an ecstatic Woodrow Wilson exclaimed, "It's like writing history with lightning."

When the NAACP and other black leaders took to the streets and denounced it, Wilson, like all good politicians, played the denial game. He claimed that he didn't really mean to endorse the film. He couldn't leave bad enough alone and added that he brought the film to the White House as a favor for an "old acquaintance [Dixon]."[20]

Griffith wasn't the only filmmaker who sniffed dollars and glory in foisting the black brute's criminal image on the public. Between 1910 and 1911, these gems graced the screen: *Rastus in Zululand, Rastus and Chicken, Pickaninnies and Watermelon,* and *The Chicken Thief.* Perhaps it was fitting and certainly appropriate that these parts were played by white actors in messy cream black face. I knew then who the real toms, coons, mulattos, mammies, and bucks were.[21]

By then, there were many whites who didn't need to read Dixon's novel or see Griffith's film to know what to do with the "half child, half animal." The year *The Clansman* was published, more than one black person was lynched, burned, shot, or mutilated every week in America. The year Griffith's film debuted—1915—the weekly lynch toll was still the same.[22]

> *Note: Many people still think that black men were lynched because they committed rape. They weren't. In most cases, they weren't even accused of rape. Even then, the apologists for lynching knew this.*[23]

V

Politicians, being politicians, seemed to feel that if the public believed that black men were inherent rapists, why spoil it with the truth? So when President Teddy Roosevelt rose to address Congress in 1906, lynching was very much on his mind. He sternly lectured, "The greatest existing cause of lynching is the perpetration, especially by black men, of the hideous crime of rape."[24]

The old Rough Rider didn't want anyone to get the idea that he was condoning lynching; after all, it would look a little odd for the man sworn to uphold the law to applaud those who broke it. He obligingly denounced the "lawbreakers." But Teddy had made his point. The *Cincinnati Inquirer* in 1911 thundered against black men for committing the "unspeakable crime" and bragged that "the mob is the highest testimony to the civilization and enlightenment and moral character of the people."[25]

Even when the NAACP's W. E. B. Du Bois bitterly called

lynching America's "exciting form of sport,"[26] Page was undaunted. He chalked lynching up to the "determination to put an end to the ravishing of their women by an inferior race."[27]

Note: Remember U.S. Supreme Court Justice Roger Taney's famous dictum in the Dred Scott case in 1857 that a black has no rights that a white man is bound to respect? Well, I was curious. If black life was so devalued and white life so elevated, were there ANY cases where whites were executed for killing blacks? A study of 15,978 legal executions since 1608 found thirty cases where whites were put to death for killing blacks. The percent is a paltry .00188 percent of the total. There are many qualifiers. Seven of the victims were slaves (property, not human beings). Several murderers were foreigners. Most of the others had white victims, too. I found only one documented case in the past half century where a white man had been executed for solely killing a black . . .[28]

The press, always on the lookout for a sensational story, read the public mood. In the crimson days before the doughboys marched off to save the world for democracy, the press milked the black beast angle for all it was worth. The *New York Times, Chicago Tribune, Boston Evening Transcript, San Francisco Examiner, Atlantic Monthly* and *Harper's* heisted the lingo from the academics and had great fun ridiculing, lampooning, butchering, and assailing black men in articles and cartoons. They were "brutes," "savages," "imbeciles," "moral degenerates," and always "lazy, lazy, lazy." The Century magazine claimed it overheard this exchange between two blacks:

Uncle Rastus: Now dat you daddy too ole to work, why don yah get a job?
Young Rastus: No! indeed ain't going to have folks say everybody works but father 'bout mah family.

Remember Uncle Rastus was a good ole darky. The young one, well. . . . The *San Francisco Examiner* put its good darky on the cartoon pages. Beginning around 1910 and continuing for half a dozen years thereafter, the Sambo series was wildly popular in America and spawned a generation of imitators.[29]

Between World War I and II, a few liberals and radicals hoped that the press and the public would knock off the crude stuff and start down the path of racial enlightenment. Black editors knew better. They were still fighting tough battles to get the major press to stop stereotyping black men. Whenever a crime was committed, if a black was involved or suspected, newspapers almost always mentioned it. In case some were slow to make the connection, they would plaster a black face across the page.[30]

Note: Blacks, as always, tried to find some humor in the situation. They joked that if a black ever wanted to get the white press to write about them, he should commit a crime and make sure the victim was white.

―――――――

The defeat of Hitler and America's ascension to superpowerdom ushered in the American Century. This was supposed to be the era that American military might and economic muscle would bring permanent prosperity and freedom to the world. It would be an era when the winds of racial change would end segregation and race hate forever.

At least that was the hope. The reality was that the old ways of race thinking, unlike old soldiers, would neither die nor fade away. While Presidents Harry Truman and Dwight Eisenhower publicly professed to support civil rights, they were frozen deep in a race time warp about black male menace/incompetence. Truman routinely cracked "darky jokes" and never got out of the Old South habit of calling blacks "Nigras."[31]

In 1954 Eisenhower had more than political reservations about the Brown decision on school desegregation. At a White House dinner party, Ike winked, nodded, and whispered to Supreme Court Chief Justice Earl Warren that he understood why Southerners wouldn't want "to see their sweet little girls required to sit in school alongside some big black buck." Neither Ike nor Warren laughed.[32]

For a short while it seemed that blacks might get a little breathing space. The civil rights movement pricked the consciences of many Americans. Congress, the White House, and the Courts, with varying degrees of enthusiasm, finally relented and eliminated legal segregation. But with the deaths of Malcolm X and Martin Luther King, the collapse of the civil rights movement, political repression, and the self-destruction of black-power radicalism, young blacks were organizationally adrift.

Recession and economic shrinkage began to wreak havoc on the black poor. Watergate may have sunk his presidency but Richard Nixon's seemingly boundless store of personal racism had much more buoyancy. He routinely peppered his talks on social issues with Secretary of State Henry Kissinger and all the other President's men with "jig," "jigaboo," and, of course, "nigger." Nixon devised a Southern strategy that stoked the fear and hostility of many whites toward blacks.[33]

In a final tour de force Nixon taught America how to speak in a code language about blacks that sounded faintly reminiscent of the Old South days. (Remember "law and order," "crime in the streets," "permissive society," "welfare cheats," "subculture of violence," "subculture of poverty," "culturally deprived," and "lack of family values"?)

Reagan didn't snore through Nixon's lesson on race ethics. He once bragged to, of all people, a black reporter how he would treat black leaders: "I said to hell with 'em." He more than meant it. By the end of his White House years, the language got rougher. The press now routinely tossed around terms like "crime-prone," "war zone," "gang-infested," "crack-plagued," "drug turfs," "drug zombies," "violence-scarred," "ghetto outcasts," and "ghetto poverty syndrome." Some in the press let it all hang out and called black criminals "scum," "leeches," and "losers." Then pictures of these black males routinely began to appear on the front pages.[34]

Note: Why drag up what happened a century ago? Many argue that Americans don't believe or do any of these things anymore.

Two young blacks, Michael James and Jackie Burden, would disagree. On December 8, 1995, they were gunned down by two white soldiers in Fayetteville, North Carolina. They were not gang-bangers, dope dealers, drive-by shooters, or carjackers. They were regular people, walking down the street minding their own business, when they were gunned down.

Officials found enough Klan, Nazi, and right-wing militia literature and paraphernalia in the soldiers' rooms to stock a hate museum. Officials had strong evidence that army bases were fast becoming hotbeds of Klan, neo-Nazi, and militia hate-organizing. Yet the army brass, local officials, and the police claimed that the murders weren't racially motivated. They were committed by two lone nut crazies.

I waited to see if federal and state officials would use the same script—"not racially motivated," "no evidence of a conspiracy"—to explain the torching of at least twenty-three black churches (known) between 1993 and 1995. Some had Nazi, Klan, and antiblack racist epithets scrawled on the charred walls. I'm still waiting.[35]

Chapter 2

The Fine Art of Black Male Bashing

I still believe Chuck Stuart pissed off a lot of people in the media. Here's why. On a dreary October night in 1989, the bloody bodies of Stuart and his pregnant wife Carol were found in the front seat of their car. It was parked in a dark alley next to the predominantly black projects in Boston's Mission Hill section. Carol Stuart was dead. Her baby died later after a C-section. Chuck, suffering from a gunshot wound to his stomach, was rushed to the hospital. On the way, a police officer who accompanied him asked him, "You see who shot you?" Chuck miraculously possessed enough of his faculties to answer "A black male."

At the hospital, Chuck kept repeating the words like a broken record: "Shot me, shot my wife, black male." The nurses and attendants thought it was a little peculiar that a man fighting for his life could say so clearly that his attacker was "a black male." These were mere trifles that Boston newspapers weren't concerned with at the time. The crime was simply too ghastly. A white, middle-class professional woman was dead and her husband was severely wounded. They were the "Camelot couple," and Chuck had uttered the three terrifying words, "a black male." The apocalyptic nightmare of black crime had finely shattered the nervous peace in suburbia.

The stampede was on. The killing, said one editor, had "sparked particular outrage." The *Boston Globe* and *Boston Herald* filled their pages with horrific stories about desperate, violence-prone young black men terrorizing the city. Men such as these were capable of anything, and the Stuart murder proved it. The *Herald* publisher seemed positively giddy at the public response: "We couldn't print papers fast enough to keep up with the demand."

The politicians weren't far behind. They whiffed a big story and jumped in with both feet. The mayor, city council members, and state legislators thundered against the lawlessness, offered big rewards for the killer(s), and promised to hunt it/them down. The Republican State Committee wasn't satisfied. It demanded that the legislature immediately reinstitute the death penalty. Republican state legislators had their marching orders and swore that they wouldn't rest until the legislature reinstated it.

Meanwhile, black Bostonians knew that there would be hell to pay. They braced themselves for the furious onslaught. It came fast. For days, dozens of police roamed the streets of Mission Hill and the surrounding black areas looking for suspects. The horror stories began almost immediately. Young black men told scary tales of police making them crawl, kneel, and lie belly down on the ground while they conducted record checks on them. Others told how police made them pull their pants down in public streets while they searched them. Dozens were hauled away for questioning. Others were arrested on a variety of charges. Some were beaten.

Eventually the police latched on to thirty-nine-year-old Willie Bennett. He was the perfect patsy, an ex-convict with a long rap sheet. It probably would have worked, except for a few doubters who didn't just read the newspapers but also read Chuck Stuart. They were suspicious of his actions and his motives. A relative who knew that Chuck was really the triggerman had also begun to talk. The noose began to tighten around him. But Chuck cheated the hangman by jumping into Boston Bay. By committing suicide, Chuck blew the lid off what *Newsweek* called the "great hoax."[1]

Note: A court later tossed Bennett's false arrest, harassment, and defamation of character suit against the Boston police department out the door. It was a nice try, but Bennett, a chronic loser currently serving a twelve-to-twenty-five-year sentence for robbery, probably knew in his heart of hearts that when the smoke cleared and the public, press, and police moved on, in the eyes of the law and much of the public he would always remain a guilty man.[2]

———

Let's take another look at the "great hoax." Suppose the doubters hadn't raised questions? Suppose a relative had kept his mouth closed? Suppose Chuck hadn't committed suicide? Suppose, suppose, suppose. Take them away and Bennett almost certainly would have been tried and convicted for the murder. If there had been a death penalty, he would have gotten it.

Was the press irresponsible in fanning the flames of hysteria and racial paranoia? The editors were in no mood to offer *mea culpas*. They were defiant and unrepentant. "Hey," they squealed, "we were just doing our job and reporting the news." "Look," they protested, "the public wanted information." "Listen," they shouted, "black men do commit a lot of crimes." In its wrap-up story on the case, *Newsweek* took a big swing at black leaders who complained about negative press reporting on the black community. It accused them of "trying to have it both ways."[3]

The point sailed way over the heads of the magazine's editors. The issue is not the coverage, it's the type of coverage. No one is telling the press not to cover crime stories about blacks, but cover other stories, too. When the press obsessively focuses on criminal acts by some blacks and excludes everything else, look what happens. Boston newspapers played the race/crime card hard, and predictably got the Pavlovian response. Politicians talked tough about law and order and scored more brownie points with white voters. The police took license to violate basic rights in the black neighborhoods. And white suburbanites were scared stiff.

Newsweek did ask one correct question: if Carol Stuart had been a black woman would the press have cared? I also ask, If Chuck had said that the murderer was a white man, would the press have run the scare stories it did run? Remember the media images of black men a century ago? Today, when editors lace their features on African Americans with terms such as "crime-prone," "crackheads," "educational cripples," "poverty-ravaged," and "gang-ridden," what has really changed?

Despite what *Newsweek* says, the media obsession with ghetto crime, drugs, gangs, and poverty titillates and scares many whites (as well as many blacks and other people of color, too). It absolves the press of the responsibility to report, probe, and find answers to why black men do all the allegedly "brutal" things they do.

Note: It was a good thing for George Bush in 1988 that much of the media didn't probe too deeply into the real causes of crime. If they had, Republican strategists could not have played the black brute image like a finely tuned Stradivarius violin. They cast escaped Massachusetts convict Willie Horton in the brute role and used him to batter Democratic presidential candidate Michael Dukakis as "soft on crime." The big lead Dukakis had over Bush evaporated faster than a disappearing act by Houdini.

Later, a bewildered Horton screamed Foul! *He claimed that he never committed the crimes that the Bush people said he did, and he was sick and tired of being everybody's political fall guy. Well. Even Horton couldn't really expect anyone to believe that he was a born-again choirboy. But even if everything Bush said about him was a big lie, Bush knew that tons of voters would believe that it wasn't.*[4]

Editors often feign ignorance that they distort the news. But many editors know that race bias is buried deep in their news and features.

How could it be any other way? The men and women who run the show in the media are hardly neutral or objective bystanders who just report the news. Their tastes, preferences, personal beliefs, values, outlook, class, money, status, and, of course, prejudices bear directly on what they consider news, and how they cover it.[5]

II

It's been that way for years. The men who trailblazed, molded, and shaped the news business were petty potentates. They answered to no man, country, flag, or even God. They had power and they exercised it with reckless abandon. In the press room, their word was law. Once *Los Angeles Times* publisher Norman Chandler bluntly asked his managing editor, "Do we have to run this? Do we have to put this in?" It was phrased as a question, but the editor knew better. It was a command.

Time and *Life* founder Henry Luce cut right to the chase, shouting, "I don't believe in objective journalism." They wanted men around them with whom they felt comfortable playing tennis, golf, or schmoozing at lunch, men with whom they didn't have to watch their language. If someone blurted out a racist or sexist wisecrack, the fellows laughed and nobody was offended because they all spoke the same language.

Washington Post owner Phil Graham golfed regularly with *New York Times* ace James Reston. *Times* heir Iphigene Sulzberger told her publisher husband Arthur (remember, she was a woman, and in those days public decisions were made by the men) to surround himself with only "fine young men, intelligent and proper" to make decisions at the paper.[6]

The pioneers are long gone but their ghosts still rattle around the editorial boardrooms. More than 91 percent of those "proper" men making the decisions about what's news are still white.[7]

This isn't to say that "proper" blacks wouldn't necessarily make the same decisions about content and coverage. If they share the same upper-crust mind-set, values, and background, like to hang out at the same country clubs and on the tennis courts, and believe that their poorer black brethren are crime-prone and derelict, the news would still look the same. In an era when the media can turn Hollywood madam Heidi Fleiss into an instant superstar, when even the barest scintilla of scandal and kinkiness can send news editors salivating, and where corporate control is in the tight hands of the mostly privileged conservative editors and publishers, stories on black achievement will still take a backseat (if that) to a juicy ghetto murder or rape story any day.[8]

III

But maybe I'm wrong. Four years after *Newsweek* gingerly chided the press for its panic reporting on the Stuart case. I made an informal survey of five of America's biggies, *Time*, *Newsweek*, the *Los Angeles Times*, the *Wall Street Journal*, and the *New York Times* for the month of August 1993.

Note: The press tossed so much public glare on the Stuart case that it sent a bad signal to some white criminals: if they get caught red-handed, it's okay to shout "A black man did it!" Of course, the press didn't invent that line. It's an American classic that's been used for decades. The press just let the world know about it.

To keep it simple, I excluded the three major 1993 domestic stories—the Reginald Denny beating trial in Los Angeles, the thirtieth anniversary of the March on Washington, and the Rodney King case—from the survey. I focused on just the "routine" daily coverage of black news. Articles appeared on crime (I stopped counting at twenty-one), welfare-poverty-homelessness (five), and AIDS (one). There were no articles on black achievement. Here's what the press did and didn't say:

Los Angeles Times, August 23, 1993, p. 1

In a multipart story on "youth in trouble," the *Times* profiled the cases of several black teens. Seventeen-year-old Gregory is one. Gregory has been in and out of detention for drug selling, vandalism, and truancy. The story line is that Gregory is not really a bad kid but was led astray by an "unpredictable father." He's a violent man who killed his wife, bought drugs from his son, and eventually deserted him. The *Times* makes only scant mention of the fact that the father was also a mentally disturbed, physically disabled Vietnam veteran.

The story did not say whether he received financial assistance, veteran's benefits, or hospitalization, therapy, and quality medical care to overcome the trauma and shock of his Vietnam experience. Despite the horrors of their experience, many Vietnam vets were discarded, forgotten or maligned by the general public as dope-smoking misfits.

A study by a New York commission on quality care for the mentally disabled found that thousands who suffered chronic emotional disorders did not receive quality in-home care and were dumped on the streets with no means of support. This might have shed some light on why Gregory's father ended up the way he did. But that was another issue. In the editor's eyes the better story was about a crime-addicted, black teen spawned by a derelict, convict black father.

New York Times, August 31, 1993, p. 1

Since the report by Daniel Patrick Moynihan on the black family in 1965, we have been constantly reminded that absentee black men have turned black families into a "tangle of pathology." Bill Clinton, George Bush, and Dan Quayle made the family a big issue during the 1992 presidential campaign. Clinton and the pack of Republican presidential pretenders, under the guise of a great welfare-reform, teen-pregnancy, and family-values debate, recycled the script in 1996. They used it as a battering ram against the evils of welfarism and big government.[9]

Anyone can make a compelling case for black male deviance and family destabilization. Here's how: Jumble income and population figures, downplay the achievements of the black middle class, and ignore the profound gender-role changes in American society. Then pretend that the Reagan-Bush-Gingrich, and yes, Clinton cuts in job, education, and family support programs benefited the poor.

But what happens when an article does try to put a positive spin on single dads who raise their kids? Howard, Fred, and Troy are trying to do that. Howard and Fred are white. Troy is black. Howard is described as a successful businessman who can afford a maid to help raise his three sons. Fred, a former army sergeant, is a UPS driver, happily raising his young daughter. Both men come off as solid middle-class guys, sans wives.

Troy, on the other hand, makes his living on a $16,000 annual income as a data-processing clerk. He says he "didn't remember his father," and "he grew up in a rough-edged neighborhood." Fred and Howard, from the impression conveyed by the article, were naturally experienced fathers. Troy was different. He was "determined to be a good father but unsure how to gain the skills."

Did the *Times* ever wonder that perhaps Troy's uncertainty about parenting was due less to his "natural" skills and more to his marginal job and low income? Howard and Fred were older men with adequate incomes and a business and a well-paying profession. This made the crucial difference in their parenting success. The *New York Times* may not know it, but there are other black men in "rough-edged neighborhoods" who are "experienced fathers." Better still, there are even some black men who don't live in "rough-edged" neighborhoods" who are experienced fathers, too.

Note: A prominent CBS programming executive "resigned under pressure"—the Orwellian corporate term for "canned"— after he cracked that black men make good late-night TV view-

ers because they are unemployed and have short attention spans. He claimed—take your pick—that his remark was a joke, misquote, lie, distortion, or journalistic invention. Okay. These things happen a lot with these guys but what made it really scary was that 116 big-name producers, writers, directors, and performers defended him. Yeah, I know they're all pals in the business, but I would have thought that at least one would have asked, "Did he really say it?" and, if so, "Did he really believe it?" [10]

Time, August 16, 1993, p. 45

Time certainly did not have men like Troy in mind in its feature on carjacking. But the pictures of the arrested young men looked suspiciously like him. They were all young black males. The reporter included the usual customary editorial flourishes using phrases like "thugs opened fire," "rolling danger," and "fuels a kind of hysteria." The reporter reminded readers that young men in the inner city are the most likely victims of violent crimes.

The problem with all this is that it had little to do with the story or the crime. In a sidebar feature, *Time* admitted that half the thefts are orchestrated by organized car-theft rings. They sell the parts to chop shops (salvage yards that pay up to $5,000 for the hot goods). Insurance companies have even gotten in on the organized thievery. They will buy parts marked up two to three times their store value.

The larceny takes place far from the borders of the ghettos. Two white professional thieves who made good livings swiping autos in Philadelphia were profiled. One was a veteran and a "good" family man. He almost bragged about his "profession." Although he was arrested nine times, he never served any prison time. In the article, the pair came off as regular though slightly crooked Joes.

Who said there is no honor among thieves?

Newsweek, August 21, 1993, p. 40

Even when the press tries to be "objective," scratch the surface a little, peer underneath, and the bias lurks. This *Newsweek* cover story, "Wild in the Streets," reports that teen violence is not just a problem of the ghetto. White suburbanites fear that they can be mugged or murdered, too, not by marauding blacks but by the kid next door (or in their own house).

The article ticks off a spate of gruesome shootings, beatings, and stabbings that have shocked suburbia. In Houston, it was a rape strangulation. In Dartmouth, Massachusetts, it was a classroom murder. In Ft. Lauderdale, Florida, it was a beating and stabbing. The culprits were white teens. *Newsweek* was the paragon of objectivity. It skipped the gore, guts, and hysteria. It made no judgments. There was no sneaky editorializing, no amateurish psychoanalysis of each killer's personality. Just the facts.

When the accounts of violence shifted from the suburbs to the inner-city "war zone," *Newsweek* loaded up. Suddenly we were in no-man's land. It was "gang-riddled South Central Los Angeles" with its "blood-splattered sidewalks" where kids "grow up to the sounds of sirens and gunshots." They live in "neighborhoods where trauma seems normal" and the "normal rules of behavior don't apply."

There's danger at every turn in this black no-man's land where wild people roam. Six-year-old Shaakara tells us about that. He lives in the no-man's land of Chicago's teeming ghetto. Shaakara describes in graphic detail how a man slashed a baby and then beat to death its grandmother. In Detroit, a nineteen-year-old tells how three of his "homies," Bootsie, Shadow, and Showtime were killed. "I saw the blood from the back of his head spread on the snow."

No one should minimize the pain and shock of seeing friends and relatives murdered whether in the ghetto or suburb. But accounts like this do just that. Are we to believe that no blood spread on the ground from the kid who was bashed in the head and dumped in a quarry by six white teens in Ft. Lauderdale? *Newsweek* never tells us. Maybe that's because their names weren't Bootsie, Shadow, and Showtime, and they didn't live among people to whom the "normal rules of behavior don't apply."

Los Angeles Times, August 16, 1993, p. B1

Michael Yocum, thirty-eight, is one of an estimated 40,000–75,000 people in Los Angeles County who on any given night prowl the streets searching for food and shelter. Even though many of these men are white, Yocum isn't. He's black. As such, he's guaranteed a featured spot in a story on the homeless.

Yocum is pictured sitting at a window with the lonely, forlorn look of a desperate man. He subsists on welfare and whatever he can get scavenging. We're told that he can't work because he has a bad back. Even if Yocum's back was in tip-top condition it might not change his plight. During the Reagan-Bush years, the unemployment rate for black men was double to triple that of white men; their earnings dropped to 74 percent of white males'.

More than one-third of the jobs lost during the 1990–91 economic downturn were lost by blacks. Asians, Latinos, and white males all gained jobs. A black male college graduate was more than two and one-half times more likely to be unemployed than a white college graduate. Men like Yocum watched while industry packed up and fled the inner city to the suburbs, taking thousands of jobs. If Yocum lucked out and got one of these jobs, he'd go into deep debt trying to pay the steep transportation costs getting there.[11]

Even so, in countless interviews men like Yocum tell sad tales of layoffs and firings after plant closings, followed by dead-end searches for nonexistent jobs. Occasionally, one of these men will turn the tables on a skeptical reporter and ask if the reporter thinks he gets perverse enjoyment sleeping under tunnels, underpasses, and bus stops in the heat, cold, and rain? Does the reporter think it's fun being preyed on by thieves and harassed by the police?

Maybe that's why one young black man I saw begging near a busy intersection in the posh Marina del Rey section of Los Angeles carried a sign that read, "I'm not a bum, addict, psycho, lazy, or stupid. I want to work." He knew exactly what many whites thought about him, and he answered back.

Wall Street Journal, August 31, 1993, p. 10

The editorial writer for the *Journal* didn't drive by that corner and see the poor fellow's sign. On the occasion of the thirtieth anniversary of the March on Washington, the *Journal* lectured —before he fell from grace—NAACP executive director Ben Chavis and—before he resigned—Urban League director John Jacobs on their "responsibility" as black leaders.

Chavis and Jacobs had raised the *Journal*'s neoconservative hackles by demanding that Washington foot the bill for a fifty-billion-dollar Marshall Plan-style domestic bailout plan for the inner cities. The *Journal* grumbled that these "leaders" should stop looking to Sugar Daddy Washington for help. It assured readers that other than a few pockets of bigotry "buried in the psyches of some Americans," racism was dead. Black folks should quit blaming whites for ghetto misery, forget about government programs, and stop haranguing corporations about affirmative action. Chavis and Jacobs would be wiser to tell their people to develop:

1) "respect for the rule of law"
2) "renewed reverence for hard work"
3) "individual responsibility"
4) "stable families"

Lazy, criminal, derelict, and immoral (sex-crazed): did the *Journal* miss anything? This would have warmed the hearts of the gentlemen-scholars of the nineteenth century who used pretty much the same arguments to explain black inferiority.[12]

IV

It's been six years since the Stuart/media debacle and more than a year since white South Carolina housewife Susan V. Smith dumped her two young sons into a lake and then latched onto "A black man did it" line to try and weasel out of it.[13]

Let's look at the tale of two Willies to see if anything has changed. One Willie is San Franciso mayor Brown and the other Willie is LAPD chief Williams. Please note that when I talk about these men I'm not talking about the Hortons, Bennetts, or boyz-N-the-hood "gangstas." I'm talking about two prominent, rock-ribbed, establishment-oriented black men.

Brown served nearly twenty years as the speaker of the California Assembly. The press cultivated the image of Brown as a combination pimp/stud/devil-may-care/near-crook. He personified the uppity black who delighted in thumbing his nose at whites. When he challenged and won the mayorship in 1995, these were the choice code words the media biggies used to describe Willie the mayor.

- *Christian Science Monitor,* December 14, p. A17:
  "Dealmaker Brown may topple incumbent Frank Jordan"
- *New York Times,* December 12, 1995, p. A12:
  "Brown loves the fast quip, fast cars, fast living and he plays politics fast and loose."
- *Los Angeles Times,* December 13, 1995, p. A1:
  "imperial style," "highly superstitious," "flamboyant politician," "pricey tastes"
- *Wall Street Journal,* December 15, 1995, p. A14:
  "political carpetbagger moves on . . ."
- *Newsweek,* December 4, 1995, p. 44:
  Its story title, "The Real Slick Willie," says it all.

Two final thoughts on Willie the mayor and the press. The *Journal* called Brown a carpetbagger. He held exactly one office for more than a quarter of a century. He didn't quit the assembly to run for the mayorship. He was forced out by term limits.

California governor Pete Wilson is a conservative Republican. Before he was governor he was the mayor of San Diego and a U.S. senator, and he made a terribly failed bid for the Republican presidential nomination in 1996. He tried for or held four offices. There were no term limits that forced him out of any of these offices. Yet if you can find any press references to Wilson as a "carpetbagger," "dealmaker," or as "imperial" in the loads of news stories on him, your eyes are better than mine.

As for *Newsweek*'s "The Real Slick Willie," I'm trying to imagine headlines that read "The Real Slick Phil" (Gramm), "The Real Slick Pat" (Buchanan), "The Real Slick Newt" (Gingrich), or "The Real Slick Bob" (Dole). In fact I don't hear the media call the real slick Willie (Clinton) "the real slick Willie" anymore.

Note: Sadly Willie Brown wasn't the only Brown who took a media beating. In the days after Secretary of Commerce Ron Brown's tragic death in a plane crash in Croatia in April, 1996, the media rightly hailed him as a talented, selfless, dedicated public servant. But much of the media that praised him in death had denounced him as a crook and demanded that Clinton fire him and a grand jury indict him when he was alive. The Wall Street Journal *labeled him the "Beltway wheeler-dealer." Other newspapers pawned off every bit of gossip, innuendo, and rumor about Brown's allegedly shady financial dealings. Brown understood that despite his personal and political success he was still under an intense racial looking glass and to some he would always be Ron Brown the "beltway wheeler-dealer."*

––––––––––

Now for the other Willie. The press honeymoon with LAPD chief Williams was brief. The signal that it was over began with veiled hints, innuendos, rumors, and much grousing from the mostly rank-and-file white police officers that the chief was incompetent, insensitive, and had lousy work habits. The city's paper of record, the *Los Angeles Times,* gleefully reported every snippet of backbiting gossip about the chief as gospel.

The carping about the chief grew to a crescendo when the

police commission accused the chief of receiving hotel and gambling perks in Las Vegas in 1994 and reprimanded him for
"lying" when he swore that he didn't.

The *Times* published in blow-by-blow detail the commission's
reprimand of the chief in his personnel file. By publishing what
at least in theory were confidential personnel records, the *Times*
walked a fine legal and ethical line on privacy rights. The chief
was no angel in all this. It appeared he did do some of things
they accused him of and was less than straightforward when
asked about them, but his image as a bumbler, liar, and near-
crook was firmly planted in the public mind.

The *Times* bloodletting didn't stop there. It continued to feed
the gossip mill with a steady barrage of unsubstantiated, uncon-
firmed, and much-denied rumors that city officials would dump
the chief at the end of his five-year term. The chief vowed to
fight on to save his job. But whether the chief could work
enough damage control to rescue his image as a badly flawed
black public servant was anybody's guess. The betting odds,
however, were that he would not be rehired for a second five-
year term in 1997.

Note: I try to be fair and give credit where it's due. Some news-
papers and networks have increased the number of stories and
features on blacks who are doing things right instead of wrong.
This doesn't mean that the media has changed its biased ways.
It just means that it is getting tired of people like me calling
their news coverage racist and insensitive and occasionally tries
to do something about it.

It's a cliché, but it bears repeating when it comes to media
reporting on black males: The more things change the more they
stay the same. It's a pity. The men and women who write these
things aren't inherently evil or malicious. Some consider themselves good liberals, sensitive to social causes and issues. Some
are even paid-up members of the NAACP and the National
Urban League, and give to the United Negro College Fund.
Some agree that they should hire more blacks (if they're quali-

fied, of course). Some have black friends and acquaintances. They don't deliberately slam black men. They don't have to.

Over time, the ancient racial stereotypes have been confirmed, validated, and deepened until they have taken on a life of their own. If editors constantly feature young black males as gang members or drug dealers and not as Rhodes, Merit, or National Science Foundation scholars because they don't believe they exist, or don't believe that they are capable of achieving those distinctions, then the news becomes a grim self-fulfilling prophecy.

Whether racial stereotypes predominate because of benign neglect or savage intent is irrelevant; the end result is the same. Many whites, Latinos, and Asians (and some blacks) shiver in terror around young black males. This gives conservatives more ammunition to decapitate job, education, and social programs, to torpedo affirmative action gains, stymie civil rights legislation, and obliterate civil liberties. It's all done under the pretense of the big black scare.

Willie Bennett knows all about this. While sitting in a cell at the Norfolk County jail, he was told of Chuck's suicide. This exonerated him. He should have been happy, but he wasn't. He said simply, "My life and my family's life have been ruined and no one is willing to take responsibility."[14]

Unfortunately, *Newsweek* and the nation's press had no answer for him or the thousands of other Willie Bennetts victimized by the fine art of black male bashing.

Chapter 3

From Slavery to the Sports Arena

I really miss Jimmy "the Greek" Snyder. I miss him so much I almost wrote to CBS executives asking them to rehire him. I always felt the only reason they fired him as a sports commentator in 1988 was because he was honest. The Greek said that blacks dominate major sports because they were "bred to be that way by the slave owner." He only said what many of the men who make the decisions in the sports profession really think about black athletes.

Note: CBS received more than two thousand letters after "The Greek" was fired. In the beginning the fans supported CBS, but hmmm. *After they thought about his words, sentiment swung sharply against CBS. Many thought, Maybe the old Greek was right. In the words of one fan, "The truth always hurts."* [1]

———————

"The Greek" has a better memory than most. During the plantation days, when the slave masters got tired of counting cotton dollars and playing bedroom footsie with the "colored" house servants, they would round up their pals and arrange a little sport. They would select two of their biggest, brawniest, blackest bucks and toss them into a makeshift ring. The masters would guzzle gallons of whiskey and rum, crack jokes, and make big wagers while the two bucks banged each other to a bloody pulp.

Before he escaped from slavery, black abolitionist Frederick Douglass watched it all with disgust, noting that "only those wild and low sports peculiar to semicivilized people were encouraged." For their bumps and bruises, the black bucks might get a little better food, an extra set of hand-me-downs and, if especially lucky, their freedom. These black bucks were the master's prize gladiators. They had to be treated a little special.[2]

The end of slavery brought a halt to the master's sporting life with his prized bucks. As free men, their services were no longer needed. Even in the formative years of major league baseball, there was just too much money and prestige involved to let them play. For years to come, the only thing black in baseball were the player's shoes. Black athletes could showcase their talents in the Negro Leagues, barnstorming through backwater towns and playing in pastures, cow fields, or ramshackle lots.[3]

In the early years of basketball, they could join the Globetrotters and play clowns, buffoons, and "Uncle Toms." A few found some glory (but no money) in football and track only because in those days they were considered bush league sports. As long as they kept away from white women, they were tolerated in boxing since it was considered a sport for brutes anyway. When Jack Johnson forgot that, the sport (and the country) KO'd him fast.[4]

Black men, however, were just too good at running, jumping, and whacking those balls. It was only a matter of time before the new masters in sport would remember them again. Jackie Robinson broke the color bar in baseball, Chuck Cooper in basketball. After that the rush was on to get as many of them as white folks could stomach at one time. Some fans grumbled. Some owners resisted. Some white players talked of boycotts. It was like trying to stop the ocean tides with sandcastles. Black players were in major sports to stay. The racial complexion of the sport had changed but the mentality of many of those who ran it, promoted it, and broadcast it didn't. They were still black performers, employed for the amusement and entertainment of the public and always bottom-line profit of the men and women who run major sports.[5]

Note: The latter is especially important. Sports is one of America's biggest cash cows. A relatively few select hands milk it for all it's worth. Here's how one black player can fill the milk bucket: During Patrick Ewing's university basketball days, Georgetown squeezed an estimated $4.5 million out of him in ticket sales, TV, publicity, and promotional revenue. The cost: a scholarship worth $48,000 and a degree. True, Ewing now makes millions as a superstar for the New York Knicks. But how many other black college ballplayers can say the same?[6]

When an occasional critic like sports sociologist Harry Edwards complained that blacks were still underpaid, underappreciated, and unaccepted as social equals, sports writers and executives quickly reminded him that slaves don't make millions of dollars, receive college educations, and live in palatial estates in the suburbs.

Edwards should shut up and be grateful. If it wasn't for sports, these guys would be selling hot clothes in Harlem, peddling dope in Watts, or carjacking on Chicago's West side. Eventually, they'd all wind up serving hard time in some joint. Edwards reminded them that some of them ended up doing that anyway once they were dumped from a team because of injury or a run-in with a coach, or fell from grace with an owner.

Edwards further reminded them that even successful black athletes were often discarded like a dirty jockstrap once their glory days were over. They did not step from the court, gridiron, or cinders into Congress or the Senate like Jack Kemp, Bob Mathias, and Bill Bradley. Yeah, there was ex-Olympian Ralph Metcalf who went to Congress, but that was another time and place, and how often did anyone mention him as a possible presidential candidate?

The way Edwards could tell what many sportsmen really

thought of black athletes was the way they were educated. How many were majoring in law, medicine, or engineering? Now how many were majoring in physical education, sports therapy, social studies or simply "undeclared"? Their graduation rate from colleges was a national disgrace.

When Edwards cracked that a high school athlete had a better chance of being hit on the head by a meteor then making a pro team he was not being tart. He was only suggesting that maybe it was time for those aspiring Jordans and Emmit Smiths in the ghetto (and their parents, too) to reexamine their priorities. There was nothing wrong with young black men spending as much time preparing for English and algebra exams as they did practicing handoffs and power-spin moves around the hoop, even if it did make some coaches mad. If they had any doubts, they should take a closer look at the fate of many of their million-dollar, All-American black heroes.

Note: From now on, when college football bowl mania strikes every year I'll think of Nebraska coach Tom Osborn and star running back Lawrence Phillips. Phillips was arrested and sentenced to probation and counseling for assaulting his girlfriend. The media, sportswriters, and women's groups howled when Osborne reinstated him to play in a big game: Nebraska's 1996 national championship bowl victory.

Phillips had barely gotten his uniform off when Osborne told him to "go pro." Osborne got his championship. Nebraska U. got its glory. In a few years we'll see what an ex-jock and coach-induced college dropout like Phillips gets when his playing days are over.[7]

II

Ask for more money. When former Los Angeles Ram running back Eric Dickerson did, many sportswriters carried on a relentless vendetta against him. They called him a whiner, overrated, overpaid, and an ingrate. They recycled old articles telling the public that pro athletes are really just grown men playing kid's sports. They're not like Joe Blue Collar who has to sweat and scuffle for his $497.59 weekly take-home pay.

Dickerson could have answered, True, but he'll make that for the next forty years with no risk of blown knees or broken arms, legs, or necks. He could have said that no one squawks when they pay Frank Sinatra or Bob Hope long dough for appearances even though their best days are way behind them. If he did say that, it wouldn't mean much. When the sportswriters got through with him, the poor guy felt like he should have paid the owners for the privilege of playing.

Overpaid, arrogant black superstar athletes can be made into pariahs in ways that defy detection. The well-traveled have-show-will-travel football free agent Deion Sanders is a case in point. Sanders took his act from the Atlanta Falcons to the San Francisco Forty-Niners to the Dallas Cowboys. He was paid a king's ransom, got a bushel of commercial endorsements, and loads of TV play. So where's the beef? There wasn't any until I noticed that a few sportswriters and announcers continually harped on his injuries. A few others constantly questioned his worth as a player. A few others incessantly reminded fans that pro football was headed to ruin because owners shelled out mints to players like Sanders. And nearly all of them repeatedly took shots at his "clownish" antics on the field.

Get injured. Darryl Strawberry, a Los Angeles Dodger before drug use and domestic violence charges did him in, and Houston Rockets player Hakeem Olajuwon know about this one. Many sportswriters called them malingerers and shirkers. They accused them of being con artists out to stick the team up for more dollars. Black men aren't like "normal people." With all that muscle and brawn, black men are supposed to be impervious to injury and pain. Even if they come armed with a dozen letters from doctors and specialists supporting their injury claim, it won't stop the owners and sportswriters from putting out the word that they're "injury-prone."

This is a polite way of saying they're damaged goods. If the black athlete is smart he'll make no big-ticket-item purchases, save his money, and plan on a speedy retirement because his days are numbered. Black damaged goods aren't kept on injured reserve or taxi squads very long. And they damn sure can't be long-term benchwarmers. Those are the quota spots reserved for marginal white players.

Be your own man. How many sportswriters still hummed "I like Mike" when they found out Jordan had something more important to do than grin at President Bush at the White House after the Bulls won their first world championship? How many gushed *oohs* and *aahs* for Air Jordan when he demanded the right to spend his money anyway he wanted? If that meant gambling on golf, blackjack, or pinochle, it was nobody's business but his own. These were the same guys who chuckled and winked at the off-the-field drinking and carousing antics of former Oakland Raider quarterback Ken "Snake" Stabler. There were no indignant articles that accused him of "damaging the sport." Naw, he was just a good ole boy having fun.

When Mike mildly complained that the sportswriters were being "unfair," they huffed that they had indulged him for years, practically made his rep for him. And they allowed him to make millions. Gee, and I always thought that the crowds mobbed the arenas, and the sportswriters greedily snapped up their complimentary press box seats to see the most exciting and entertaining athlete in sports.

Note: This item was buried on the second-to-the-last page in the sports section of the Los Angeles Times *on Saturday, October 9, 1993. After an investigation of Mike's gambling activities, NBA commissioner David Stern announced there was "absolutely no evidence that Jordan violated league rules." I guess the sportswriters must have missed this, since few of them mentioned it in their columns. If Stern had found some evidence that he had . . . need I finish?*

In any case, all the hubbub plus his father's murder took a toll. Jordan took a sabbatical from the court to sort things out. A year and a half later a less airborne Mike came back. The fans and sports establishment cheered again. But Mike probably knew that if he ever slipped, those cheers could again just as easily turn to jeers.

―――――――

Be outspoken. Football's Jim Brown, baseball's Reggie Jackson, and basketball's Bill Russell were proud black men who had more on their minds then just X's and O's, RBIs, and rebounds. They also had opinions about race, politics, and how their people were treated in America. This was a bad mistake. The press branded them "black militants." Yes, they got their money and fame. It was hard not to begrudge them that since they were the best athletes in their sport. But the sportswriters laced their columns with innuendos that the sport might be better off if they shut up and played ball.

Tragedy strikes. For years Magic Johnson rode sky-high in the sports saddle. He had the slavish adulation of a city, the unbridled respect of sportswriters, the devoted admiration of sports owners, and the endearing attachment of corporate advertisers. In November 1991 that all changed when he announced that he had contracted HIV. The doors slammed, and rumors, innuendos, accusations, and taunts flew hot and heavy. Magic quickly read the handwriting on the wall and quickly chucked it all. But Magic had too much charm, goodwill, and resiliency to stay down.

Four years later the Magic show was back in business. He returned to the pro game. The fans went wild, sportswriters applauded, sportsowners approved, TV ratings soared, and Magic became the only sports figure ever to appear on the covers of *Time, Newsweek, Sports Illustrated,* and *U.S. News & World Report* (Secretariat and O.J.—for the wrong reasons—made the covers of three) on the same date. Magic's redemption and triumph seemed complete—except for one thing. The privileged and wealthy men that make the rules in the world of corporate money and power were not waving "Welcome back, Magic" signs. All his old corporate chums made it clear they had no immediate plans to use him again as their visible TV pitchman.

Magic continued to lose millions in product-endorsement income. He was still a fallen idol with a huge image problem.[8]

III

Even when black athletes act like deaf mutes on social issues, don't raise a stink about salaries, behave like choirboys, and have cast-iron constitutions, chances are that sportswriters will still use racial doublespeak when they talk about them and white players.

I take my cue from "Monday Night Football." I've watched nearly every game, starting with the first game between the New York Jets and the Cleveland Browns in September 1970. Over the years, I compiled these code words from the sports chatter of the announcers:

White Player: Heady.
Black Player: A burner, a speedster, or "can motor."
WP: Good work habits.
BP: Moody, a head case.
WP: Cagey, disciplined.
BP: Erratic.
WP: A project (this means that the team's owner is willing to spend time and money waiting for him to produce.).
BP: Raw talent, but doesn't live up to his potential.
WP: Fearless, courageous.
BP: Hears footsteps.
WP: Aggressive, a hustler.
BP: A real animal.

Occasionally, an announcer got excited and forgot to use racial doublespeak. This happened to Howard Cosell in 1983. He called Washington Redskins wide receiver Alvin Garett "a little monkey." Cosell promptly got called out on it. If he had simply called him a "burner," "aggressive," or even a "scooter," he'd have been home free. In the following years, sports announcers knew they were being watched. So they were on guard not to make the occasional silly, racially tinged gaffes. But that hardly meant that racial nirvana had enveloped the sports booth. The bias simply changed forms.[9]

During the 1996 Fiesta Bowl game, nearly every time troubled "girl friend-batterer" Nebraska running back Phillips touched the ball the game announcers reminded millions of viewers about Phillips's "troubles," "difficulties," and "problems" with the assault case and his critics. They openly speculated whether he might be damaged goods to the pros. And all poor Phillips thought he was in the game for was to pack the pigskin and help the Big Red lock up number one.

Note: *The critics continued to beat up on Phillips after the Rams made him their first-round draft choice in 1996. Yet they were strangely silent about his white teammate, Christian Peter. The giant defensive tackle apparently did more than sack the opposing teams' quarterbacks. Between 1991 and 1994, Peter was charged with harassing and assaulting a woman in a bar, attacking a former Miss Nebraska, twice raping a Nebraska coed, and threatening the life of a parking-lot attendant. He also faces a federal sex discrimation suit. Peter got brief media mention only after the New England Patriots drafted him and then dropped him because of his sex and violence record.*

My computer search turned up twenty newspaper articles that specifically mentioned Phillips's off-the-field woes. Despite Peter's misdeeds, there was exactly one on him. Peter is a white athlete with an off-the-field record that made Phillips look like an altar boy. I wonder how the sports establishment missed this?

So bring back "the Greek." He made the game so much simpler. He never kept the blacks guessing about where they stood. That's why Jackie Robinson said in his autobiography, "I never had it made."[10]

Chapter 4

Doing the Wrong Thing by Spike

I think Spike knew that they would hate him. The *they* are numbers of film critics, studio executives, black conservatives, some black militants, and black feminists. In recent years, they've all ganged up on the fellow for his alleged sins.

With many studio executives and film critics, it was pure hate and envy from day one. They called him arrogant, abrasive, and a jerk. They really didn't like him because he's an uppity nigger that speaks his mind and happens to be damn good at what he does.

Yes, I know that they bankroll and promote his films. Some critics even claim that if it wasn't for Hollywood, Spike would be shining shoes in front of a subway station in Brooklyn. Wrong! Hollywood didn't make him. It makes money off him.

His first film, *She's Gotta Have It,* was a no-budget film made with lots of credit cards and much arm twisting of friends and relatives to help out. *School Daze* was a low-budget, mom-and-pop shoestring job, too. When the films raked in the cash, the studio executives really took notice. They loosened the purse strings, but not much.

Jungle Fever and *Do the Right Thing* became huge hits. Compared to the legion of other stinkers that Hollywood releases and routinely writes off when they bomb, these two films were still nestled deep in Hollywood's low-rent district. They were controversial, however, and there's nothing better than controversy to get Hollywood panting, tongues wagging, and cash registers jingling.

Then Spike and Hollywood found Malcolm X. Why not? After five years, Malcolm had been glorified by rappers, hyped by street T-shirt and cap hawkers, seized by the fashion industry, packaged and sanitized by Madison Avenue, and defanged politically by politicians like Dan Quayle and celebrities like Madonna. Studio executives hoped that *Malcolm X*, the film, might even bag some of the crossover crowd. Many hip-hop whites, Latinos, and Asians were also wearing X hats and T-shirts. Someone even spotted Bill Clinton sporting an X cap.

Warner Bros. upped the cash. But it was still wary. That's when the conflict began. They complained that Spike was spending too much money and taking too much time with "the project." The film critics eagerly saw it as a chance to take more cheap shots at him. They called him a whiner, complainer, and a spoiled brat. The few extra million dollars Spike was asking to finish the film was bare pocket change to the studios. *Far and Away* cost $60 million. *Honey I Shrunk the Kids*, $40 million. *Patriot Games*, $65 million. *Batman*, $55 million. The studios didn't bat an eye at the costs.

They happily shelled out $12 million to Arnie for his role in *Terminator II* and $8 million to Tom pretty-blue-eyes Cruse for his part in *Far and Away*. Their salaries could have practically bankrolled Spike's film.[1]

Note: *Black filmgoers buy an estimated one out of four movie tickets and black films, made on a dime, routinely gross anywhere from $15 to $60 million. If Spike got far more money than any other black director has gotten to make a film, it is not a credit but a discredit to Hollywood.*[2]

Warner Bros., embarrassed, finally piped down and ponied up the rest of the bread when Lee got his pals Oprah, Air Jordan,

Magic, and Bill Cosby to kick in some spare change. The film critics merely bided their time. When the film was released they got their revenge. They called it a flop before the projectors were barely warm. Some self-proclaimed liberal critics found nothing redeeming about Malcolm's life, the film, or—though they didn't say it directly—the filmmaker.

This is the same bunch who turned into deaf mutes after the eternal revivals of *Gone With the Wind* and *The Birth of a Nation,* or gushed over them as "classics." *Gone With the Wind* seared into the memories of generations of schoolchildren the myth of the happy-go-lucky, faithful darky. *The Birth of a Nation* glorified the Ku Klux Klan. And who said the South lost the Civil War? Zippity doo-dah![3]

Note: The Birth of a Nation, it seems, has had something of a rebirth. During one week in April, 1996, both The Movie Channel and the Turner Classic Movie Channel aired the uncut version of the film. There were no protests or angry press editorials. Before it aired on TMC, two commentators made brief, tepid and almost apologetic remarks about the film. They said little about the racist content of the film and nothing about the massive NAACP protests against the film when it was originally released in 1915.

With the murderous resurgence of The Aryan Nation, The Order, neo-Nazis, the Klan, and Skinheads, not to mention the proliferation of ultraconservative Militia and Patriot groups, I would think somebody would say something about the potential danger of films like this. Just another sign of today's times.

II

Anyway, Spike could handle them. He never had any illusion that they would ever accept an arrogant, skinny-assed black man in their circle.

Black folks were another matter. The black conservatives complained that Spike was whipping up race hatred and inciting violence in his films. As a guest, I had to sit through nearly an hour on one radio talk show listening to one of them denounce Spike for showing the tape of the Rodney King beating and burning the American flag in the opening scene. The scene took about a minute or so. I wondered what he did to amuse himself during the rest of the film's three hours and twenty minutes?

Instead of backing him, black militants backbit him. They yelped that he would defile Malcolm's sacred image by turning him into a dope-dealing second-story thief, desperate to get under a white woman's skirt. They weren't buying Spike's sensible explanation that he was not making an underground documentary for arty-farty revival houses but a real commercial movie, for real theaters and real moviegoers.

They didn't listen when Spike said that the film would erase the image of Malcolm as a hate-filled fanatic who called whites "devils" and introduced thousands of people (including many young blacks) to Malcolm's life and ideology. They forgot that one of the qualities that made Malcolm great was his ability to admit his mistakes and reevaluate his ideas. He was able to look deep into the scarred abyss of his soul and America's soul and wage an intense struggle to change both.

Some black feminists ragged on Spike AND Malcolm. They claimed that Malcolm was really a sexist and that the Nation of Islam treated women like kitchen help. They didn't think Spike portrayed women much better in his films. *She's Gotta Have It* supposedly proved that. They twisted it around to make Nola, the lead character, a sexually exploited Barbie doll for her men. She wasn't. When one of her lovers pesters her to tell him if he's as good as her other two lovers, she says, "That's the dumbest thing you've said." He pleads some more: "But I love you." She knows better. "You're not in love with me. You're in love with my lovemaking. Don't mess it up." This doesn't sound to me like a woman who's a dingbat plaything of the fellows.[4]

III

Then there was Malcolm. To call him a male chauvinist is like calling a caveman dumb when he can't master an advanced

MAC Quadra computer system in one sitting. Malcolm was a product of his times and thinking. Feminism for black men and women during Malcolm's life was not even a word then, let alone a full movement or ideology. Forget what Malcolm said; how did he treat Betty Shabazz and his children? Betty had no complaints. She said Malcolm was a kind, considerate, loving parent and husband. Malcolm did not treat her or regard her as an inferior. Spike took pains to show that Betty was a strong, independent woman. Malcolm respected and appreciated her.

Note: The women in the Nation of Islam didn't think it was a badge of inferiority when the brothers called them "sister" instead of "bitch," and did not abuse or beat them but made them feel honored. My guess is there are a lot of black women who would like the same thing today.

———

After his break with the Nation, Malcolm rethought many of his ideas about the role of black women in the movement. Three months before his murder he said, "I am proud of the role that women, our women, have played in the freedom struggle and I am in favor of them having full freedom because they have made a greater contribution than many of our men."[5]

IV

That's not all that bothers me about Spike's black critics. They are the same folks that were stone silent or drooled over films like *Boyz N the Hood, Menace to Society,* and *Dead Presidents.* They proclaimed the young black filmmakers geniuses for capturing the gritty reality of the "hood." "Geniuses"? Take a closer look. They glorify guns, cash, and dope. They reduce the English vocabulary to a vile stream of "Goddamns" and "motherfuckers." They savage black women as "bitches" and "hos."

Was it an accident that the same Hollywood film critics who made a growth industry out of mugging Spike went gaga over these films? Why did they think it was so great to show young blacks cursing, fighting, and killing each other? Or maybe they were just happy that the filmmakers didn't blame the "white establishment" for the crisis of the ghetto.

That was Spike's problem. He played it to close to the vest. He thought that black folks occasionally might want to see themselves as something other than crooks, clowns, and charity cases on the screen. He believed that he could sneak films with positive messages through the Hollywood cracks. That's quite a feat working in the industry most religiously wedded to the notion of turning sex-violence-stereotypes into cash. The temptation is always there to backslide and give the public Hollywood's warped vision of the "hood."

After *Malcolm X*, Spike tilted in that direction with a couple of films *Clockers* and *Girl 6*, that do the drug/ghetto/gangsta and gratuituous sex antics number. Still, I hope that Spike regains his touch and keeps doing the right thing in his films, even when others don't do the right thing by him.

Chapter 5

Thomas, Tyson, and Tall Tales

I never believed Anita Hill. Not because I thought that she deliberately lied about Deh Judge, Clarence Thomas. Nor because the issue of sex victimization is trivial.

I don't believe her because she raised the issue at the wrong time, in the wrong place, and with the wrong people. I don't believe her because to this day she and many feminists use Deh Judge as a club to bludgeon the nation on the issue of sexual victimization, but do not treat William Kennedy Smith, Robert Packwood, big-wheel politicians, prominent corporate executives, and a legion of Hollywood actors, entertainers, and sports stars in the same way.

Note: Sex discrimination is illegal. Yet despite a Supreme Court ruling that proclaims sexual "intimidation, ridicule and insult" illegal, when and what constitutes sex harassment is still subject to wildly varying interpretations by individuals, courts, and state laws.[1]

The polls consistently showed at the time Deh Judge was on the sexual hot seat that the majority of blacks didn't believe her either. That included many black women. The way some of the black women in my office reacted told me why they didn't believe her. The day Anita testified, they were livid. Two were so angry they were crying. These are not stupid, naïve women. They were not mad at Anita because she broke the "code of silence" within the black community on sex abuse. They would not tolerate for a second any kind of sexual abuse or violence against women. They did not agree with Deh Judge's personal or political conservatism. They didn't really give a damn whether he was confirmed or not.

They were mad at Anita because they believed that black men and women should work and struggle together. They were mad at Anita because they believed she was being used by whites to get at a brother. Their anger tells why many blacks sniff hypocrisy in the issues of feminism, gender issues, and racism, issues that some civil rights leaders, feminists, and black radicals deftly dance around. I'll come back to this.[2]

Note: The racial/gender double standard starts with the perception of unfairness in the media. Example: In an eight-month study of reporting on domestic violence, Fairness and Accuracy in Reporting (FAIR), a media watch-dog group, caught the San Francisco Chronicle and the Examiner with its journalistic pants down. They found that the newspapers "underreported or trivialized domestic violence as unexpected, out of character or inexplicable" when the assailants were white males. Would FAIR find fairness or the same double standard in the reporting of domestic violence at other newspapers throughout America?[3]

II

Deh Judge. When Anita said he talked about "Long Dong Silver" and pubic hairs on Coke bottles, and made nasty gestures, Deh Judge didn't need his law degree from Yale to know he was in deep shit. Sexual perversion and black men instantly rattle ugly tremors in the hidden recesses of the collective psyche of many whites. Deh Judge sweated. For an instant, he saw all the painstaking years he spent grinning, buck dancing, shuffling, and playing the good nigger flushed down the stool. He could make Heritage Foundation speeches until the cows came home. He could shout all the content-of-character-not-color-of-skin drivel he wanted. It couldn't flush his reputation back up.

Deh Judge didn't have to think about his response. He screamed that this was a "high-tech lynching of an uppity black man." If white Americans and the senators believed Anita, and many secretly did, including the ones who claimed they didn't, Deh Judge would have been run out of Washington on a rail. But when you're black and conservative, politics makes strange bedfellows. If Anita had been white even that wouldn't have saved him. Instead of being confirmed as a sitting judge, Deh Judge might have been sitting in front of a judge.

Feminists loudly complained that the senators gorillaed Anita. They were right. If Deh Judge had been a white man, they wouldn't have had to worry. Nobody would have believed her anyway. Hill-Thomas would have been parlor gossip quietly buried behind closed doors.

If Anita was roughhoused by the senators, it wasn't simply because she was a woman. It was because many white men didn't think of her as a woman. The old plantation myths applied to her, too. Slave women were thought to be loose, hot, and promiscuous, and they couldn't wait to dash from the fields to some big black buck's (or slave master's) bed. During slavery, there was no law on the books to protect black women from rape or sexual abuse.

Later, some of the best and brightest black actresses and entertainers paid their dues playing sultry harlots, whores, and tramps who hopped from bedroom to bedroom. Nina Mae McKinney bumped and grinded on the dance floor in *Hallelujah*. Lena Horne pranced around in *Cabin in the Sky*, tempting the fellows. Dorothy Dandridge was an amoral gold digger in *Carmen Jones*. Fredi Washington in *Imitation of Life* was the tragic mulatta suspended between two worlds. White men then could never love or accept her as a true woman, especially if they believed she spent her life in a perpetual hunt to do the "wild thang."[4]

Note: Some might retort, Didn't Congressman Mel Reynolds's conviction for talking dirty on the telephone and other assorted sex crimes with a young black girl contradict your theory that black women have less worth than white women or men in the eyes of the law? No. Reynolds was guilty and there's no defense or justification for his acts. But there is the strong suspicion that the government targeted Reynolds (and many other black elected officials) for racial reasons and not simply their misconduct. If not, then how come the government did not throw the same legal book at three other congressmen who were accused of sexual misconduct? One, like Reynolds, was a Democrat. Two, unlike Reynolds, were Republicans. And all three definitely unlike Reynolds, were white.[5]

Anita really shouldn't have had to worry. Black women don't have the monopoly on dirty images. Tell me how many of the workmates in the stable of Hollywood superstar madam Heidi Fleiss are black women? Most of the high-priced prostitutes are white. They don't ply their trade on the streets but in expensive salons and mansions. They rarely get busted because their clients are some of the richest, most powerful men in America. Unlike black women, they don't call the women that service them whores or tramps, but madams, call girls, escorts, and professionals.

The same goes for welfare. Many Americans take it as an article of faith that lazy, irresponsible black women lie around all day in the ghetto making babies with lazy, irresponsible black men and then run to the welfare office and expect public tax dollars to take care of them. If I said that far more lazy, irresponsible white women lie around all day in backwash, rural towns making babies with lazy, irresponsible white men, and then run to the welfare office and expect public tax dollars to take care of them, some would suggest I need a psychiatric attendant.

While neither stereotype is true, white women do make up the bulk of welfare recipients.[6]

Note: This was buried in the pages of the Life Style section of the Los Angeles Times *in October 1995: "Sixty percent of births outside marriage in 1993 were to white women and seventy percent to women older than 20." The next month this was buried even farther back: "The figures on out-of-wedlock births showed a significant increase among affluent, white well-educated working women." The government report shattered two myths/stereotypes. Now will the press, the public, and policymakers start talking about ignorant, immoral, irresponsible, well-to-do white women making plenty of babies and problems, and creating an economic and tax drain on America?*

III

While Anita made it close for Deh Judge, she didn't win. Desiree Washington did. She had some things going for her that Anita didn't. She didn't wait for nearly a generation to accuse Mike Tyson of sexually abusing her. She was in Indiana, a state more Southern than Northern. She was young, apparently innocent, and a beauty queen. Iron Mike wasn't a staid, conservative, politically connected black man. He was big, black, brawny Iron Mike, the modern-day reincarnation of Bad Nigger Jack Johnson. Tyson was a Brooklyn street tough, ex-thief, reform school bully, and wife beater. He had a lengthening rap sheet that included car wrecks and sexual assaults. What sane person couldn't believe that Tyson couldn't commit rape. RAPE![7]

His only hope was to throw himself on the mercy of history. Following emancipation, Southern states gradually put rape laws on their books. Theoretically, they applied to black women, too. But everyone knew better. For nearly a century, there were few cases of any white man being convicted of raping a black woman. To this day, there is absolutely no record of any white man being executed for raping a black woman. And there never will be.

A Supreme Court decision in 1967 made rape no longer a capital crime (unless there was a murder). Two years later a Florida court finally sentenced a white man to life imprisonment for the rape and murder of a black woman. This didn't necessarily mean that the law or public opinion had become any more enlightened.[8]

A black coed was assaulted and raped at St. John's University in 1991 by three white students. In a feature story, the *New York Times* agonized over the student's plight. It quoted the defense attorneys extensively, played up the solid middle-class background of the students and parents, and dismissed the defendant in one line as "dropped out of St. John's after the incident." INCIDENT? It was a rape case! There was only a brief quote from the prosecutor, and no comments from her friends or relatives.[9]

The year before, a white woman was "wilded" by young blacks in Central Park. Just for fun check out the *Times* coverage of that case and see if you spot any differences.[10]

Tyson could pray that the court would remember that black women for most of this century weren't thought of as real women, but whores. If he had been the average black man and Washington the average black woman, he might have skipped away scot-free. If he had been a politically connected, well-heeled white man like William Kennedy Smith, he would have skipped away scot-free. But he was Iron Mike.

Note: *When I point out the gender/racial double standard in the media, law and public policy, and attitudes, someone always says, "Well, yes, but the circumstances aren't the same." Or my favorite: "You're not comparing apples to apples." I will.*

Two Hollywood actors. Two men. Two cases of domestic violence. Two arrests. The difference: Billy Dee Williams is black. Sasha Mitchell is white. Williams: Bail $50,000; charges immediately filed; national news coverage. Mitchell: Initial bail $25,000; undetermined whether charges were immediately filed; no national coverage. Was Williams's alleged crime more severe? You decide. Mitchell was a professional kick boxer, charged *with kicking and hitting his pregnant wife on two occasions. Williams was charged with simple assault.*

The point is not to dump on white men and certainly not to justify, rationalize, or try to excuse sexual assault, abuse, or harassment by black men (or anyone else). The point is to show that crimes committed by black men are often blown up, magnified, and sensationalized for the public. Crimes committed by nonblack men are hidden, masked, and obscured for the public. Making sex crimes appear to come exclusively with a black face hijacks what should be a color-free gender issue and puts women at even greater risk.[11]

In defending himself against Anita during the confirmation hearings, Deh Judge explained the problem he and Iron Mike had. "If you want to track through this country in the nineteenth and twentieth century the lynchings of black men, you well see that there is invariably a relationship with sex, an accusation a person can't shake off."[12]

Deh Judge wasn't through: "I cannot shake off these accusations because they play to the worst stereotypes we have about black men in this country." Feminists and civil rights leaders went ape. To them, it was blasphemy for him to compare what Anita said about him to a lynching:

1) He was an "Uncle Tom."
2) It was self-serving, cynical, and opportunistic.
3) Anita was not a white woman or a lynch mob.
4) He was still alive.

Based on the Deh Judge's pathetic performance on the Supreme Court bench, one could certainly make an airtight case against Deh Judge on one or more of these points. But Deh Judge still made his point. Black men weren't lynched because they raped white women. In most cases they weren't even accused of a crime. Black men were lynched for the same reason they were demonized as lazy, irresponsible, sex-crazed brutes and defectives: to maintain white control, power, and domination. Rape was a serviceable myth. And Southerners joyfully reminded everyone that black men were brutes toward their own women, too. That was Deh Judge's problem. It was Iron Mike's, too.

IV

The myth of rapacious black male sexuality is still one of America's most durable and deadly stereotypes. Contrary to popular view, it far predated slavery. In the early 1500s, European explorers in West Africa were fascinated with black sexual practices. One explorer called the penises of Mandingo tribesmen "burthensome members." Another marveled at their "large propagators." Later, Shakespeare couldn't resist talking about those "lustful" darkies. The black Othello had googoo eyes for the white Desdemona. As such, she was always in grave danger from "the gross clasps of a lascivious Moor." [13]

Note: Listening to the way the courtesans plotted and expressed their racial/sexual hatred of the Moor in the 1995 film version of Othello, I thought the great bard had updated his masterpiece.

The white planters didn't have to read Shakespeare to figure out they needed more than whips, guns, laws, slave patrols, dogs, and the militia to keep the darkies in line. They needed a myth, one that they could elevate to national hysteria. Black hypersexuality was perfect. They convinced themselves and most whites that those bestial black men with their large propagators were after their dainty white women.

For a time during slavery, North Carolina, Pennsylvania, New Jersey, and Virginia even stuck a few laws on their books prescribing castration for any black man who attempted to rape a white woman. They quickly erased the laws. It had nothing to do with stricken consciences. Too many blacks running around with lopped-off private parts were damaged goods and bad for business.[14]

Defeat in the Civil War didn't change much. Southern politicians and the former planters working under the cover of the KKK and other white supremacist organizations launched a successful campaign of racial terrorism that rolled back the meager Reconstruction gains. When they finished, blacks were free in name only. To make sure it stayed that way, they revived the old myth that the bestial black men with "large propagators" were after white women. Southern newspapers and magazines were filled with lurid, unsubstantiated accounts of white women being threatened by black men.

The politicians got into the act. In 1900, Clifton Breckinridge, diplomat, and U.S. minister to Russia, issued this dire warning to the nation about the black race: "When it produces a brute, he is the worst and most insatiate brute that exists in human form."[15]

The learned men weren't far behind. They had already made their compelling case for black inferiority; now they took dead aim at black hypersexuality. In 1903, Dr. William Lee Howard triumphantly announced in *Medicine* that the "brutes were driven to fits of sexual madness" because of "the large size of their penis." Unlike the white man's penis, the Doc assured his readers, the black brute's penis lacked "the sensitiveness of the terminal fibers." Skip the mumbo jumbo; the learned man was simply saying that no women were safe from black men with their massive, throbbing dicks.[16]

The theme of black male sexual menace was now a wide-open, lucrative field for researchers and popular writers. Yale sociologist William Graham Sumner applied Darwinist theory to social studies and became the rage among academics, politicians, and business leaders. In *Folkways,* published in 1907, Sumner assured a doting public that blacks were driven by only two things: fear and sensuality. It made them "cowardly, cringing, cunning and false, and at the same time fond of good eating and drinking and of sensual indulgence." Sumner's writings influenced a generation of sociologists, social researchers, and academics.[17]

Their research, writings, and opinions had deadly consequences. The number of race riots and lynchings sharply rose immediately after World War I, and the nation's top business leaders and academics refused to speak out. Southern sheriffs, judges, and local elected officials refused to prosecute lynchers. In Congress, the unholy alliance of Southern Democrats and Northern Republican conservatives torpedoed more than a dozen bills to make lynching a federal crime.

Presidents Warren G. Harding, Calvin Coolidge, Herbert Hoover, and Franklin D. Roosevelt—liberal or conservative, Republican or Democrat—it made no difference. They all refused to support antilynching bills in Congress. Southerners raged that a federal antilynching law was an unconstitutional abomination. When a few conscientious Northerners said it wasn't, the antilynching opponents got rough, promptly trotted out the rape myth, insisted that they were duty-bound to protect white womanhood from the menace of the black rapist, and got their way.[18]

Note: Over the past century Congress has been asked a zillion times to make lynching a federal crime. It didn't. And it still hasn't.

––––––––––

By the start of World War II, scientists and scholars had pretty much discredited the old racialist theories of black inferiority. But black sexual depravity was another matter. In 1942, the renowned scholar William Montague Cobb tried to make what he considered a well-intentioned effort to disprove the myth of black hypersexuality. His science failed him. In the *American Journal of Physical Anthropology* he produced five archaic studies (one was published during the Civil War), including his own, that purportedly proved that black men had bigger penises than white men. No scholars took him to task. Mercifully, Cobb didn't mention anything about "sensitive terminal fibers." The meaning was still the same. Women, watch out![19]

Note: The initiation process in this kind of thinking often starts early. Two white boys were joking about sex. I was standing nearby. Suddenly, one turned to the other, pointed to me, and said, "Let's ask him about doing it. They know all about that stuff." I was in the sixth grade.

During the 1940s and 1950s major newspapers in Chicago and New York bombarded readers with scare stories on sex crimes allegedly committed by black men. The NAACP and black editors were outraged and demanded once again that the press knock it off. While some Northern editors agreed to stop the hatchet jobs, their brethren in the South were having none of it. In 1956 the editors of Southern newspapers were nearly unanimous in their defiance of civil rights laws because, as they warned, it would lead to the "eventual amalgamation of the races, meaning miscegenation, intermarriage or whatever you want to call it." The "it" was the ancient and eternal fear of black men having sex with white women.[20]

Some laugh at this stuff now, but many Americans took it seriously then. During those years, thousands of black men dangled from trees, were roasted on bonfires, or were riddled with bullets because of the theories of the learned men, the ravings of politicians, and the fears of the public. This was the extracurricular stuff. When the mobs played out, the states took over. From 1930 to 1981, 455 men were executed for rape; of that number, 405 were black men. They were put to death on the flimsiest evidence, mostly the word of a white woman. It was nice and legal then, and it still is today.[21]

In Dallas, researchers noted that the rape of a white woman brings a sentence that averages ten years, a black woman two years. This doesn't just happen in hang-'em-high Texas. The findings have been duplicated in dozens of other states. The issue is not income or gender but race.[22]

Note: If the press and the public can chatter on into the next millennium about the real or alleged sex crimes of Thomas, Tyson, Reynolds, et al., then how about devoting more than one or two days' worth of front-page news to the real or alleged serial/mass, rape/murder, sexual hate crimes of Glen Walters,

Charles E. Rathbun, and James Acremant? Surely, the public has a right to know about them, too.[23]

V

It took time, but Iron Mike finally figured all this out. He said in an interview from prison in 1993: "Michael Jackson and Michael Jordan—like myself and many other black entertainers and celebrities with high profiles—are under attack and every black in the world should offer support. White society hates us just as much as they hate ordinary blacks." Tyson may have been sincere or merely borrowing a page from the Deh Judge's book and playing on the racial sympathies of many blacks.[24]

But then maybe I should indulge him since it was virtually preordained that he would be a marked man the day he stepped out of the Indiana Youth Center. He went to Harlem for a welcome-home celebration and was met by a line of chanting demonstrators demanding that he "apologize" for his "crimes" and "sins" against black women. He had barely put on a boxing glove when a chapter of the National Organization for Women warned him that if he fought in New Jersey they would picket.[25]

Note: Poor Mike got no peace. While sitting at a New York nightclub having a drink, minding his own business, a patron took off her clothes and offered to do "anything" he wanted. Tyson was so spooked by it all that he pleaded for her to "understand what I've been through" and put 'em back on.[26] *A few weeks later, yet another woman accused him of assault at a suburban Chicago nightclub. Stay tuned!*

Many black women did not have to possess the wisdom of Solomon to see that men like Deh Judge and Tyson were being targeted for alleged misconduct or crimes while nonblack men accused of the same crimes or misconduct skipped away untouched. They understood the brutal fact that the issue is first and foremost race. The painful truth is that many working-class black women reject, or are wary of, feminism because they're suspicious of white women. They see feminism as a movement of, by, and mostly for middle-class white women.

They know many don't accept them as equals or fight hard against racism. Many black feminists should know this. Some call themselves "womanists" and try mightily to distance themselves from some of the racist antics of some feminists. Others talk themselves blue in the face trying to get feminist organizations to fight hard for issues that impact black women and other women of color.

Those issues go way beyond the issue of sexual harassment. In America, race, not gender, has always been the driving force behind black female oppression. Black women were captured, shackled in slave ships, suffered illness and starvation, and were fed to sharks during the Middle Passage because of race, not gender. Black women were worked, sold, beaten, and killed during slavery because of race, not gender. Black women were lynched, burned, shot, and beaten during the lynching era because of race, not gender. Black women were relegated to poverty, peonage, and ghettos because of race, not gender.

Today, black women make less and are treated worse then anyone else in America because of race and gender. The old adage still applies that there are two kinds of females in this country, colored women and white ladies, and the only time colored women become ladies is when they are cleaning ladies.[27]

Many feminists wage passionate and honorable battles for abortion and stronger laws against domestic violence and sexual harassment. This is fine. But many black women don't see them waging the same relentless battles for domestic wages, welfare rights, and increased funding for job, skill, and educational training for black and poor women. Where would Anita be today if, instead of beating up on Deh Judge, she had demanded more funding and expanded programs for family planning clinics; more treatment facilities and better quality care for mothers and infants who suffer alcohol-, crack-, and AIDS-related diseases; fair pay and equal rights for domestics; and wages for housework?

Where would she be if she had crusaded for the press and

police to take seriously the incessant serial killing of black and poor women, as well as stronger police action, and laws against rapes and physical assaults on black women (by white and black men)? Would women's groups march her around the country and heap hefty speakers' fees and awards on her? Would they call her the Ida B. Wells of the twentieth century or the Rosa Parks of the 1990s? To her credit, I think that Anita has grown from the experience with Deh Judge and has tried to broaden her reach to hit hard on these crucial issues.[28]

Feminists and civil rights leaders waged war against Deh Judge before he wrote one opinion yet turned into deaf mutes on the unholy Nixon-Reagan trinity of Supreme Court Justices Antonin Scalia, William Rehnquist, and Anthony Kennedy, who wrote dozens of opinions savaging civil rights, civil liberties protection, women's rights, and abortion.

Note: Here's how silly it got during the Thomas confirmation hearings: a prominent black female California state senator, while raging against Deh Judge, declared she'd rather see a white racist on the bench than Thomas. There's an old saw that you can march, picket, protest, harass, and call white racists racist and make them feel guilty enough to change their evil ways. It's a good theory but somehow it never works that way.

––––––––––

Black women don't have to be feminists to fight against sexual abuse and for equal rights, equal respect, and dignity. The best proof is Hill and Washington. Pre-Deh Judge, Anita had no problem calling herself a Republican and conservative. Washington was prancing around the stage in Indianapolis in a skimpy bathing suit with dozens of other black women, trying to cop the Miss Black America crown. Feminists hate these events. They claim these pageants turn women into fetishes, commodities, and sex objects. They are right. The problem is that every time the event sponsors think about getting rid of them the women contestants say no.

There's something else some feminists and civil rights leaders refuse to admit about blacks, men and women. They are basically conservative. I'm not talking about the political pandering of black conservatives such as Shelby Steele, Thomas Sowell, Oklahoma Congressman J. C. Watts, Allan Keyes, Deh Judge, or the new pack of Deh Judge wannabes.

I'm talking about conservative in their values and ideals. They have been thoroughly shaped (okay, for the radicals, indoctrinated) by the American experience. Forget what the racists say. From slavery to the present, hard work, thrift, religion, family values, business, and self-help have been trademarks of Black America. Blacks are America's most native sons and daughters. The blood of their sons and daughters has drenched every domestic and foreign battlefield. They have rejected all "isms," including communism, socialism, progressivism, Peace and Freedom partyism, and Libertarianism.[29]

They have been among the biggest cheerleaders for the two-party system. When *Black Enterprise* magazine asked blacks "if their hopes and aspirations were the same as the white middle-class" 61 percent said "yes." The only reason more didn't agree is because despite all the faith of their fathers, America eternally finds nasty little ways to remind blacks that they are still "niggers."[30]

Note: It was radical chic during the 1960s for black and white revolutionaries to anoint the black masses as "the revolutionary vanguard." I, and many others, listened to them, believed them, and got into trouble. We should have listened and believed our parents and grandparents. They were neither revolutionary nor the vanguard. They always preached about religion, country, moral values, and basic rights. Period. They were the true bellwether of what black folks really thought.

The forty or so academics and activists that *Black Scholar* magazine in 1992 invited to speak out on Anita and Deh Judge generally missed most of this. They skirted the issues of conservatism, black resistance, and/or indifference to feminism, racism in the women's movement, black male sexuality myths, and class divisions among blacks. The majority of them bashed Deh Judge because his views were wildly out of line with the "civil rights–progressive" agenda—in short, theirs.[31]

Politically, I and Deh Judge are intergalactic light-years apart. I can challenge his views and protest his abominable rulings. In fact, I consider myself duty-bound to urge others to do the same. But I don't have the right to tell him he can't have those views. The black critics don't either. When they do they become thought police, self-appointed guardians of truth.

The truth is that many black men and women, for better or worse, have more in common with Deh Judge and Tyson (and mainstream American thinking) than with feminists and academics.

These blacks didn't pay much attention to the intellectual theorists. They knew intuitively that something was wrong. They knew that the system was treating these two black men differently. This is why they didn't believe Anita.

Chapter 6

Ain't I a Nigger, Too?

"I don't mind someone calling me a nigger if they call me to go to lunch, too." I knew comedian Paul Mooney was trying to get a laugh when he said that. After all, his job is to make people laugh and normally he succeeds. That afternoon, I appeared with Paul and two other black writers on a popular radio talk show in Los Angeles. The subject was racial hate words.

When Paul, who loudly declared that he is not offended when whites call him a nigger, made his little joke, the other two blacks laughed. I didn't.

Note: If I had the power, I'd make it mandatory that the Def Comedy crowd that yuk it up at the MF, N, H, and B word jokes go back and watch the old videos of Moms Mabley, Dick Gregory, Godfrey Cambridge, Nipsy Russell, and the older Richard Pryor. They were true artists who made people laugh without demeaning themselves or their people. A Slappy White sampler: "My landlord said he's gonna raise the rent. 'Good,' I said, 'cuz I can't raise it.'" "They sent the black astronaut up at night. They figured if there was any night life, he'd find it."

These comedians were part of the real golden age of African-American comedy.[1]

———————

Maybe I was feeling a little too "sensitive" that day. (Isn't that what some whites tell blacks when they object to a racist slur?) I was thinking about the conversation I had with my son a week earlier. I had heard him greet one of his buddies who had called with "Yo nigger, what's up."

It wasn't the first time that I heard him say that to one of his friends. In the past I ignored it. I knew it was the way many young blacks talked to each other. The word "nigger" is part of their hip jargon. They aren't particularly troubled by the odious significance of the word. This time I was. I asked him why he used it. He shrugged and said that everybody uses it. "If that's true," I asked, "then what if one of your white friends calls you a nigger? Is that okay?" He was silent.

We both knew that it was not acceptable for a white person to call him a nigger. When any white person, especially a celebrity or public official, slips and uses the word or makes any other racist reference, he or she will hear about it from outraged blacks. Ask Cincinnati Reds owner Marge Schott and sports personalities Al Campanis and Jimmy "the Greek" Snyder.

The double standard that my son and other young blacks apply to whites, but reject for themselves, is now coming back to haunt them. Many young whites, like blacks, casually toss the word around.

Not long ago, a friend found out how casually. He and two young whites were in an elevator. Suddenly, one of the whites jokingly called his friend a nigger. It didn't matter to him that a black man was standing there. Was it racism? Was it cultural insensitivity, or just plain ignorance on his part? Did he realize that many blacks find the word offensive?

Probably not. He was dressed in the latest baggy style. In the crossover world of hip culture, he's almost certainly heard many blacks call other blacks "nigger." I'm also pretty sure that he's heard black comedians and rappers sprinkle the word throughout their rap lyrics and comedy lines. Rapper Easy E has virtually made a fetish out of the word. He put it in the title of one song and then rode it to the top of the record charts.

Some black writers go through lengthy gyrations to justify using the word. Their rationale boils down to this: the more a black person uses the word, the less offensive it becomes. They claim that they are cleansing the word of its negative connotations so that racists can no longer use it to hurt blacks. Comedian-turned-activist Dick Gregory had the same idea some years ago when he titled his autobiography *Nigger.* Black writer Robert DeCoy also tried to apply the same racial shock therapy to whites when he titled his novel *The Nigger Bible.*

Many blacks say they use the word endearingly or affectionately. They say to each other, "You're my nigger if you don't get no bigger." Or "That nigger sure is something." Others use it in anger or disdain: "Nigger you sure got an attitude." Or "A nigger ain't shit." Still others are defiant. They say they don't care what a white person calls them; words can't harm them. Funnyman Paul Mooney doesn't have a problem with this.

Note: Def Comedy bigwig Russell Simmons has an answer for stuffed shirts like me: "Twenty years ago 'nigger' was self-defeating. When we say 'nigger' now it's very positive." Really. And just what magical change happened in America in twenty years that made society treat blacks as more than niggers?

The black "N" word defenders miss the point. Words are not value-neutral. They express concepts and ideas. Often, words reflect society's standards. If colorphobia is one standard, then a word as emotionally charged as nigger can easily reinforce and perpetuate stereotypes. The word nigger does precisely that. It is the most hurtful and enduring symbol of black oppression.

II

Nigger derives from the Spanish word *negro,* or black. Its original root is the Latin word *niger.* Even a cursory trace of the history of Western attitudes toward black reveals that before the slave trade, Europeans considered the color black repugnant.[2]

The *Oxford English Dictionary* defines black as "soiled, dirty, foul, malignant, sinister, horrible, wicked, a sign of danger and repulsion." White is defined as "purity, virtue and honor." In Shakespeare's *Othello,* Emilia groans to Othello, "O, the more angel she/And you the blacker devil."[3]

The early European traders and explorers in Africa filled their diaries and journals with weird tales about the supposed animalistic and heathen practices of the Africans. To them, the black Africans were an alien people. It was only a short step from this to calling them subhuman. This provided the slave trader the mental margin needed to debase blacks and turn them into property. In Western language and thought, the words "Negro" and "slave" soon became synonymous with degradation, while the words "Christian," "free," "English," and "white" meant the exact opposite.[4]

"Nigger," variously spelled, crept into the English language in the seventeenth century. In 1625, a Rhode Island law decreed, "There is a common course practised among English men to buy negers, to that end they may have them for service or slaves forever." During slavery, blacks were commodities to be bought, sold, and traded for labor and profit. Beyond that, their lives had little value.[5]

Okay, so I opened the book quoting Huck's exchange with Aunt Sally in *Huckleberry Finn,* but I just have to use it again since Mark Twain captured the total worthlessness of black lives during slavery. Aunt Sally asked Huck why he was late arriving. Huck lied and told her that his boat had been delayed:

> *Huck:* "We blowed out a cylinder head."
> *Aunt Sally:* "Good gracious! Anybody hurt?"
> *Huck:* "No'm killed a nigger."
> *Aunt Sally:* "Well it's lucky; because sometimes people do get hurt."[6]

In other words, to Aunt Sally "niggers" ain't people! Emancipation did little to alter this thinking. For nearly a century, "separate but equal" was enshrined in American law and custom and blacks were banished to the outer margins of American society. When Dr. Martin Luther King led civil rights marches in Chicago in 1966, many whites shouted at him: "I wish I were an Alabama trooper, because then I could kill a nigger legally." King later remarked that he had been called nigger so often by whites in Chicago, he began to wonder if he had a new name. In any case, King certainly knew that his life meant nothing to them.[7]

Note: Here's another thought for the Def Comedy crowd. The word "nigger" didn't work in reverse for Muhammad Ali. During the Vietnam War he shouted the great line, "No Vietnamese ever called me a nigger." He refused induction. The fans turned against him. The boxing world slammed the door on him. The government indicted him. It cost him three of his best years as an athlete. The experience taught Ali that while no Vietnamese ever called him a nigger, many Americans still did.

King's experience was hardly unique. A writer passing a group of white children playfully pelting some black children with rocks asked one, "Why are you throwing rocks at those children?" The youngster innocently replied, "Mister, they ain't children, they're niggers."[8]

Before World War I, America's major magazines and newspapers continued to treat blacks as social outcasts. Early issues of *Atlantic Monthly*, the *Century*, *North American Review*, *Harper's*, the *Chicago Tribune*, the *New York Times*, the *Boston Evening Transcript*, the *Cincinnati Enquirer*, and the *Indianapolis Journal* didn't just savage black men as clowns, criminals, and crazed sex maniacs. They also routinely referred to them as "nigger," "niggah," "coon," and "darky."[9]

The NAACP and black newspaper editors waged vocal campaigns against this racist stereotyping. Black scholar W. E. B. Du Bois frequently took white editors to task for refusing to spell "Negro" with an upper-case "N." Du Bois called their policy a "conscious insult" to blacks. In that era, being called a Negro was a matter of pride and self-identity.[10]

There were more deadly consequences. According to the NAACP, from 1880 to 1968, 3,445 blacks were lynched or burned to death in America. (This is the official figure; many suspect that the number is much greater.) For many their only crime was their color.

Black men aren't lynched or burned anymore but the quantum leap in hate crimes nationally is strong proof that racial violence is hardly a thing of the past. The majority of the attacks are still aimed at blacks. And "nigger" is the favorite racist epithet that vandals plaster on the walls of black homes and businesses.

III

The "N" word has also left psychological scars on past generations of black children whom American society treated like racial untouchables. Some years ago, one hundred black elementary schoolchildren were asked "When did you first discover that you were a Negro?" One little girl replied, "At a white neighbor's house the other children drank from a dipper, but when I asked for a drink, she said 'You're a nigger, and we don't allow niggers to drink from that dipper.' "

Another child responded, "One day a little boy called me a nigger. Since then I have thought of myself as a Negro and not just another person."

That was the idea. In spite of this, many black folks managed to turn what was intended as a badge of shame into a mark of pride and accomplish great things. This is one reason why we're still here today.

Another responded to the question in this way: "When I asked for a hamburger in a cafe, the man told me that he was sorry that they didn't serve niggers. This told me that I was a Negro and couldn't act like whites."[11]

Today that's changed. Blacks can go anywhere and eat all the greasy hamburgers and French fries they want to their heart's discontent. But the message hasn't changed. They still can't act like whites. Former and now resurrected Washington, D.C., mayor Marion Barry forgot that. He thought he could lie, cheat, and take a little white powder. When he got caught, he and some black leaders squawked that white politicians do that and much more and get away with it. If they do get caught, they get hand-slap sentences and are not mauled in the press.

Black leaders should have listened to what the young student said years ago. They can act like white men, but they won't be treated like them. I should add that many blacks look at black politicians not as politicians but as leaders and advocates to represent their interests and to challenge and confront institutional power. If they take bribes or commit crimes, they betray the trust of blacks. Their screams of racism should fall on deaf black ears and they shouldn't be blindly defended let alone treated like martyrs.

Here's another example. In Los Angeles some young blacks acted like the four white cops who beat up Rodney King. The blacks beat up white truck driver Reginald Denny. Two of them languished in jail with extortionate bail and court-appointed attorneys while the press lambasted them as gang-bangers, thugs, and hoodlums. When the legal dust finally settled, one of them was sent on a fast track to state prison with the maximum sentence.

With the four cops, the judges bent over backwards to grant them low bail, full legal assistance, and favorable rulings. All the while, they busily promoted their books and became media celebrities. A jury with no blacks acquitted them in state court of nearly all the charges.

When two were finally convicted in federal court, the presiding federal judge, Arthur Davies, was not willing to concede an inch. He described them and their families in almost idolatrous terms. He ignored the pleas of federal prosecutors to toss the book at them and barely blew a featherlight page at them. They luxuriated at a minimum-security federal prison, aptly called "Club Fed."[12]

A solid core of conservative politicians in Washington and Los Angeles treated them like conquering heroes when they were released. They planned welcome-home parties and raised bush-els of cash for the appeal of their sentences. The Supreme Court not only agreed to hear their appeals, but a few justices openly expressed their feeling that the two cops had suffered enough.[13]

The young blacks that beat Denny forgot one thing: if they act like white men, especially the ones that wear uniforms and badges and commit crimes, they won't be treated like white men. Again, I'll add that if they commit crimes, they should not be blindly defended let alone treated like martyrs either.

Note: During an interview on a national radio program, I asked this question: if former Joint Chiefs of Staff chairman and some-time presidential candidate Colin Powell had been tooling around Lakeview Terrace instead of Rodney King that March night, when it came time to kick some black ass would those cops have stiffened and saluted or whaled away on him, too? The host shot back that the general wasn't driving ninety miles an hour, stoned on PCP. He, like many others, swallowed hook, line, and sinker the fable used by the cop's attorneys to justify the stopping and beating of King. There was not a shred of proof that King did any of this.

I admit it was hyperbole to toss in Powell. However, the endless procession of prominent black politicians, businessmen, professionals, entertainers, and sports figures that have told hor-ror stories of experiences with police should more than prove the point that no matter how much clout, cash, or connections a black has, he is still considered a nigger to some.

Novelist Richard Wright, in his memorable essay "The Ethics of Living Jim Crow," remembers the time he accepted a ride from a "friendly" white man. When the man offered him a drink of whiskey, Wright politely said, "Oh, no." The man punched him hard in the face and said, "Nigger, ain't you learned to say 'sir' to a white man?" The pain from the blow would pass, but the pain from the "N" word would stay with him forever.[14]

Maybe that's why comedian Richard Pryor told an audience that he would never use the word "nigger" again. The audience was stunned. The irreverent Pryor had practically made a career out of using the word in his routines. Pryor softly explained that the word was profane and disrespectful. He was dropping it because he had too much pride in blacks and himself. The audience applauded.[15]

Paul Mooney, Easy E, my son, and anyone else who thinks it's hip to call someone a nigger should go rent the tape of that Pryor appearance.

Chapter 7

The Way Things Ought Not to Be, Rush

I would never call Rush Limbaugh a big fat idiot. Besides, one writer already did that.[1] I will, however, say mega dittos to big fat . . . I mean Big Rush for telling Americans the truth about the "black problem." This shouldn't surprise anybody. Big Rush is a self-proclaimed genius. He has a magnificent talent for reducing complex issues to code words and barbed zingers. Big Rush says blacks are in the lousy shape they're in for two reasons. One, "The federal government has assumed the role of the wage-earning father" for blacks. Note the juxtaposition of "wage-earning" and "father." It bears importantly on the second reason.

Two, "62 percent" of all black babies are born to single black women. The result; "There are no role models for young blacks." Since Big Rush doesn't consider dope dealers, drive-by shooters, gang-bangers, and derelicts as "role models," black folks, says Big Rush, are stuck with a bunch of pickaninnies running around waiting for the next handout from their Sugar Daddy in Washington.[2]

Note: Ignore the "62 percent." According to the 1990 Census, 43 percent of black homes were single-parent households.[3]

As always, Big Rush pulls figures from a hat, tosses them out, and never cites a footnote or reference to support his point. One group has even sicced a truth squad on him to blow the whistle on his whoppers. But when the subject is irresponsible black men, you don't need a truth squad to figure out that the only thing they're good at is freeloading and making babies and problems. Big Rush dusted off the century-old myth of the irresponsible, shiftless, lazy darky, spruced it up, and spit it back to us.

II

He should thank the government. In 1965, it resurrected the modern-day version of the myth. That was the year Watts exploded, blacks escalated their demands for jobs and justice, and more started listening to Malcolm X's recorded speeches. Lyndon Johnson was at his wit's end trying to figure out why blacks could be so ungrateful for all his Great Society munificence. He demanded answers.

Enter Assistant Secretary of Labor Daniel Patrick Moynihan. Johnson told him to explain their bizarre behavior. Moynihan doggedly studied the stats, figures, and the charts. Instantly, it became clear. Johnson was barking up the wrong tree. He thought that spending millions on jobs, education, housing, social service programs, and passing civil rights laws could buy social peace. For all the good it did, the government might as well have tossed the money into a black hole.

The real problem, said Moynihan, was the black family. It was a wreck. Moynihan figured that one in four homes was without a father. The black single mothers left to fend for themselves were getting poorer and more desperate. All the health, education, and welfare programs in the world couldn't change that. Just get those daddies back in the home and everything would be fine.[4]

But three out of four fathers were in the home. And many of those were desperately poor homes, too. Moynihan didn't explain why. I always wondered about his research method, which pointedly fingered black men as the root of "Negro deviancy." Did Moynihan control for income, education, and professional and family background to make sure that he was comparing middle-class blacks to middle-class whites? Or did he skew the numbers by comparing ALL blacks to the white middle class? When black family experts put controls in, they found absolutely no differences between father absenteeism rates in white and black middle-class families.[5]

Note: Here's an intriguing project for a sociology grad student. Collect income, welfare, and household stats on poor whites and compare them with the income, welfare, and household stats of the black middle class and see how poor whites stack up on poverty and father absenteeism.

This might have spoiled Moynihan's hypothesis. Social scientists always hate that. Still, there was just enough doubt raised about the report that Johnson decided to table it. But the media didn't. With Vietnam turning into a quagmire, black radicals screaming "Get whitey!" and cities from Detroit to San Francisco burning, the story of black family dereliction was just too good to pass up.

III

By the 1980s, the Reagan revolution kicked into high gear and the nation's racial mood turned even uglier. The media decided the time was right to resurrect the old derelict darky myth again to explain the growing army of black poor. Soon the airwaves and newspapers throbbed with gloomy stories about the "vanishing black family." Much of the media didn't dwell too much on the economic devastation caused by Reaganism. A good story to editors is like a hypothesis to scientists: they don't want it spoiled.

One thing, however, should spoil it. The Great Communicator stripped away job, housing, and education programs. He sabotaged unions and deepened the rust on the traditional auto, steel, rubber, and oil-refining plants that provided high-paying, union-secured jobs for many blacks. Before that, black men did not have a chronic unemployment rate double that of white males. And young black males did not have a triple or higher unemployment rate than young white males. The majority of black men were in the home.[6]

Reagan, however, didn't screw things up by himself. Many state and local officials dutifully took their cue from Washington and imposed iron-clad income limits on welfare recipients. If there was a man in the house and he brought in dollars, no matter how meager, the family in the eyes of welfare bureaucrats looked like Rockefellers and Vanderbilts. Their payments were slashed or cut off entirely. It might have been cheaper to keep her, but it wasn't cheaper to keep him. The doors in many black homes started to revolve and some black men marched out.

That in itself did not cause the black family to plunge into hopeless ruin. There was never any hard evidence that boys raised in one-parent families were being groomed as high school drop outs, drive-by shooters, dope dealers, and gang-bangers. If some were, it was not because of absentee fathers but because of absentee income.[7]

Also, many black men who did abandon the home did not entirely abandon their children. A few honest researchers found that black men are far more likely to acknowledge their children, visit them frequently, and provide some money, clothes, and food for them. This in part explains why far fewer black women throw themselves on the mercy of the court to collect alimony and child support than white women. (The other explanation is racism in the legal system.)[8]

There is something else: Black guys aren't the only ones vanishing from homes. A lot of white guys are, too. The days when Ozzie could stroll home after a hard day at the office and expect to be greeted by a beaming Harriet, with apron, smile, slippers, dinner on the table, and a spic-and-span house are dead. That's because American society has undergone profound technological, social, and economic changes. This has radically changed the family (especially women). Women have to work. Many are better educated, hold jobs in higher professions, make more money, and are independent. Even if they wanted to, and many don't, they wouldn't have the time to be cheerful housewives. They expect and demand that men pull their share.[9]

Note: Do you really believe that every white American family resembled Ozzie and Harriet during the "golden fifties"? If you do, I have a rain forest in the Gobi Desert to sell to you. Ozzie was an authoritarian who badgered Harriet, spent virtually no time with David, and browbeat Ricky. Writer David Halberstam understood exactly why Ricky later in life battled through a wrecked marriage and drug problems: he was the "unhappy product of a dysfunctional family." In The Fifties, *Halberstam tells all about the all-American fraud of Ozzie and Harriet.*[10]

IV

Maybe I should pardon Big Rush for being a little ignorant of this history, some of this happened before his time. But Big Rush should take a break from horsing around with his chums at the Institute of Advanced Conservative Studies, leave the friendly confines of his studio, and drive through any black neighborhood. He can do it at high noon on the weekend. The muggers don't operate as well at that hour. He should look past the guys hanging out on the corners and go to a park, playground, cultural event, or church activity. He will see many black men with their wives or significant others and children at play, at work, or just relaxing.

Who are these guys? They are barbers, plumbers, teachers, electricians, doctors, lawyers, accountants, engineers, policeman, mailmen, firemen, and so on. They want the same thing for their children that white fathers want, a better life.

This might be too burdensome for Big Rush. In his megaseller,

The Way Things Ought to Be, Big Rush spent considerable time trying to resuscitate Ronald "my hero" Reagan from Sleepy Hollow. Big Rush thinks he's the true people's champion. He is the man on the perennial white horse who rescued America from the Satanic clutches of the "liberals."

Then there's the Limbaugh Lexicon, a dim-witted collection of Limbaughisian slop complete with racist and sexist code words, stock lines, and idiotic slogans. Buried in this mess, Big Rush mentions only four men. I already told you who one is. The other, former New York governor Mario Cuomo, is there for reference. The other two are black men, Jesse Jackson and "General" Dinkins, better known as former New York mayor David Dinkins. The "General" is dispatched quickly as the "hapless, ineffective mayor of New York, a tool of every liberal group one can think of." In other words this ignorant darky couldn't have bumbled through his four years as mayor without help from white carpetbaggers. (Southerners hated carpetbaggers. They were considered the liberals of their day.) Big Rush kills two birds with one stone here.[11]

And then there's the good Reverend. Big Rush is a little sneakier here. He doesn't take Jackson on directly. He does that in many other places in the book. He pokes fun at him for the way he talks. Now Jesse does sometimes do strange things with the king's English and he has been roundly and justifiably criticized for his scattershot, have-issue-will-travel photo-op style of leadership. But a lot of folks in high places lead from the seat of their pants and butcher the language. This includes, if I remember correctly, his own "hero." But that's different. They don't speak "black English" like "those people."

Note: Ozzie and Harriet update—Do you really believe that the families of the big-gun Republicans still resemble Ozzie and Harriet? Newt Gingrich demanded a divorce from his first wife on her sickbed, and some say skipped child-support payments. Bob Dole admitted in an interview that he just wasn't spending enough time at home with the family, and asked for a divorce from his first wife. Phil Gramm's mother was married five times. Gramm divorced his first wife. The luckless-with-cupid Big

Rush bailed out of two marriages and has tried his luck a third time.[12]

Oh, well, this is a good place to leave Big Rush with the real truth about the black family: a majority of African Americans still live in households; a majority of these are family households; a majority of family households are married-couple households.[13]

Since I'm not a "ditto-head," Big Rush will pooh-pooh talk like that. He will continue to tell everybody who'll listen that I told you so.

Note: Thankfully there are still a few who aren't listening to him. Once readers took a gander at his follow-up tome See, I Told You So *and realized that they had already seen his tired act in print, the book free-fell faster than a blown-out rocket from the best-seller charts.*

Chapter 8

Minister Farrakhan or Adolf Farrakhan?

I know what Adolf Hitler and Nation of Islam leader Louis Farrakhan have in common: Jews. For nearly a decade, Jewish organizations have branded him the "black Hitler." How did Farrakhan beat out George Lincoln Rockwell, the original Mr. American Nazi, for this dubious distinction? Why does his name conjure up gruesome visions among Jews of burning flesh, Zyklon B gas, firing squads, open pits, and emaciated bodies in death camps? Could a black man in America have that much diabolical power? Farrakhan doesn't and never will in America. Many Jewish organizations and leaders know that. But that's not the point. Many Jews think that he does. And many more are frightened that he could.

II

Blacks always assumed that many Jews hate Farrakhan because he criticized Jewish organizations and religious practices in his speeches. There's more. Jewish organizations don't regard Farrakhan as simply a raving anti-Semite. He's also the symbol of Jewish rage against blacks. They are mad because they feel betrayed. They worked hard to build SNCC and CORE during the 1960s. They gave money, time, resources, and advice to the civil rights movement. They mourned Michael Schwerner and Andrew Goodman, who gave their lives in Mississippi for black freedom. They fought to break down barriers in unions and corporations for blacks.

They are mad because after doing all this, blacks kicked them out of their organizations, denounced Israel, supported the PLO, called them racists and ghetto exploiters, and accused them of concocting plots and conspiracies. The Minister was the ultimate insult. Since many blacks liked his message, Farrakhan became the symbol of their rage.

But the rage against him has become a fixation. Many Jews mistakenly view the black experience through the prism of Europe. They forget that the pogroms, Bunds, pales of settlement, Cossacks, peasant persecutions and Nazi death camps were products of the ancient European hatred and fear of Jews. The black experience is shaped by the whip, the cross, and the rope of American bigotry. Blacks have never had the power or the desire to oppress or exploit Jews. Their fight has been for justice and empowerment. When a black man preaches the message of empowerment, many blacks will embrace him no matter who it angers.

III

When Farrakhan came to Los Angeles on September 12, 1985, Jewish leaders, politicians, and the press fumed, threatened, cajoled, and denounced him. They also denounced then Mayor Tom Bradley and local black leaders for not denouncing him. In a pompous editorial, the *Los Angeles Times* raked him over the coals for "vicious bigotry," "raw racism," and "destructive religious intolerance."

Note: The Times *admitted that the audience applauded loudest when Farrakhan "reached out to the Jewish community with a*

*word of conciliation." To dwell on this would have blown their
script.*[1]

This guaranteed a huge gate. Farrakhan was a black man under
attack. Instead of the usual seven thousand or eight thousand,
sixteen thousand people showed up. Farrakhan served his pur-
pose that day. He was the Blackman that personified all evil.
That's all the press allows Americans to see and hear about
Farrakhan. They believe that he exists to trash Jews.

Eight years later, in October 1993, Farrakhan was again in
Los Angeles for a major speech. He talked exclusively about
building peace between the black gangs and stopping black-on-
black fratricide. The message was positive and supportive. He
did not mention the word "Jew" once. There was no opportunity to demonize him. Jewish leaders, politicians, and the press
ignored him.[2]

IV

They didn't ignore him for long. In December 1994, Farrakhan's
national spokesperson Khalid Muhammad opened the door
wide open for attack when he delivered a speech that attacked
not only Jews but practically anyone else that didn't agree with
the Minister. It was the politics of paranoia taken to the nth
degree, and Farrakhan wisely played Pontius Pilate and washed
his hands of Khalid (indefinite suspension) for the moment. But
Farrakhan unwisely didn't stop there. While he disavowed the
messenger he avowed the message and said that essentially
Khalid spoke the truth. Clinton, Congress, the public, and the
press were off to the races again. They had another field day
slamming Farrakhan as America's number-one "hatemonger."
Farrakhan and his attackers were now locked in an endless
dance of acrimony.[3]

*Note: Some cynics said that the politics of acrimony meant more
recognition and cash for both sides. When some Jewish organi-*

zations raised the anti-Farrakhan red flag, the donations and contributions poured into their coffers. This paid for the huge full-page ads they rushed into the pages of the New York Times *denouncing Farrakhan. (Unfortunately those same ads seemed to be conspicuously missing denouncing Skinhead, Nazi, Militia, and Aryan Nation hate acts and atrocities against blacks and Jews, not to mention Pat Buchanan's backhanded compliment of Hitler—"an individual of great courage [and] extraordinary gifts"—as well as other anti-Semitic taunts in his earlier [?] days.)*

On the other side, when Farrakhan waved the anti-Jewish red flag, his prestige and status among many blacks soared even higher into orbit. This also translated into more cash for the coffers. Again, I'm only repeating what the cynics said.[4]

———

The volatile mix of Farrakhan and Jewish organizations could not co-exist for long in the same space without sparks flying. The Million Man March in October 1995 kindled them. The march goals seemed innocuous enough. Farrakhan was asking black men to atone for their errant ways, get on the stick, and start cleaning up and empowering their communities. He did not attack the government, corporations, the press, or Jewish organizations. He demanded that black men cut crime, be responsible family men, respect the laws, build pride, encourage self-help, and register to vote. On the surface these were themes that smacked of good ole Americana values and traditions and could even bring a smile to the Reagan-Gingrich-Buchanan crowd.

For a brief moment I thought that the event might pass largely unnoticed and unattacked by the press and Jewish leaders. I should have known better. They couldn't resist the urge. On the eve of the march they pounced and hurled the usual charges at Farrakhan: "anti-Semite," "hatemonger," "divisive element," and so on. It was Los Angeles, February 1985, all over again. Whatever the numbers—which almost certainly would have been much smaller than Farrakhan might have gotten at the march if they had left him alone—were doubled, tripled, maybe even quadrupled. The attacks guaranteed a huge gate.[5]

The Farrakhan assailants had one last hope to blunt the messenger and dilute the message, and minimize the potential political significance of the event: try to reverse the gate. The National Park Service gave it the good ole college try. It said there were only 400,000 at the march, But even Ray Charles and Stevie Wonder could see that this was a lie. The march organizers went armed with aerial photos, charts, maps, and measurements to the Park Service. They made the case for their million. They almost got it.[6]

The revised count put the number at 850,000, with a 25 percent margin of error. The march organizers took the margin of error in their favor, officially claimed a million-plus, and declared victory. For Farrakhan it was his finest hour. He seemed to have been coronated as the titular head of black America. The polls showed that for the moment at least he was black America's main man.[7]

But Farrakhan had a problem. Many blacks also made it plain that they still regarded the Nation as stuck in the tight straitjacket of religious dogma and sectarian ideology. Some blacks were plainly worried that Farrakhan might indeed be the anti-Semite and racial bigot that the Jewish leaders said he was. If true, they were hardly willing to trade one kind of racism for another. Farrakhan had the big job of trying to find allies among mainstream black leaders and prove that the Nation of Islam could broaden its programmatic reach to all segments of black America.[8]

The burden was clearly on his shoulders to make liars out of everyone who said he was evil incarnate. Many hoped that he wouldn't do something rash to squander the goodwill the march had built up among many blacks. They were more than willing to give him, his leadership, and to some extent his philosophy the benefit of the doubt and rally behind him when he was under assault.

However, just when Farrakhan seemed on the verge of coming in permanently from the leadership cold, shortly after the march he embarked on his "World Friendship Tour." It took him to Nigeria, Iran, Iraq, and Libya. Some of the goodwill vanished and a lot of blacks bought the Clinton line that he was "cavorting with dictators." Even those blacks who ignored or dismissed this as political rhetoric were still hard-pressed to explain what his visit to these countries had to do with the struggle and plight of black America. After all, the leaders of these countries are accused of jailing, torturing, and murdering dissidents and in the case of Libya and Iran are strongly suspected of supporting terrorist groups.[9]

Note: Farrakhan evidently had some doubts about his fate on his return to America. He expressed concern that he would be accused of violating every statue on the book against trading and consorting with declared enemies of the United States and would be indicted and arrested.[10]

No matter what the outcome of the long-running Farrakhan/America passion play, he can't win. He symbolizes the hateful black man who stirs hidden paranoid fears in many whites and some blacks about blacks. Mention the name "Hitler" and it touches deep revulsion. Mention the name Farrakhan and it does the same. It's the perfect match made in hell.

Chapter 9

Why Are They Waiting to Exhale?

I have a confession to make. Author Terry McMillan was holding forth in 1992 onstage in the main reading room at the San Francisco Book Festival and I didn't know who she was. From the rapturous gazes on the faces of the several hundred women in the room, I knew she was important. Many of them tightly clutched to their breasts copies of her monster best-seller *Waiting to Exhale*. I had vaguely heard that the book loosely dealt with four black women who shift through a motley bunch of losers and deadbeats trying to find a "good black man." One reviewer called it "a tough love letter" for black men.

This made me uneasy. I edged closer to the stage to listen. As she read excerpts from the book, she waved her hands, cocked her wrist defiantly on her hips, frowned, pouted, and laughed. The crowd loved every minute of it.

During the question-and-answer period, several dozen women scrambled to the floor mikes. Terry snapped out answers firmly and with authority. Then someone asked the inevitable question: "What do black men think of the book?" Terry didn't miss a beat. "Yeah," she huffed, "they don't like it, but that's their problem." They laughed and applauded.

Toward the end, a young black woman asked her if she planned to write a sequel to the book. Terry paused for a moment, laughed, and said, "No, the women are all married and happy now." The questioner glided away with her copy locked in a death grip and with a heavenly glow on her face. The audience laughed and applauded.

I didn't. Her answer gnawed at my gut and wouldn't let loose. Later, when I read *Waiting to Exhale,* I knew why. Three of the suffering four women—Gloria, Bernadine, and Robin—in their rage called black men ugly, stupid, prisoners, unemployed, crackheads, short, liars, unreliable, irresponsible, possessive, and old and set in their ways.[1]

They weren't talking about the black men they dated, screwed, and loved. They weren't talking about the men they heard their friends, relatives, acquaintances, mothers, and maybe even grandmothers talk about. They weren't talking about the men they read about in books or saw on TV. They were talking about *all black men!*

If the four black women were now happily married, they must have found black men who were handsome, intelligent, not convicts, employed, drug-free, tall, truthful, dependable, sharing, mature, and flexible.

Why didn't Terry want to tell the world about them? Did she think that black America is a world without black fathers and responsible black men? And that black men were the eternal menaces to society? She didn't. When an interviewer asked her for the umpteenth time if the book was a black-male-bashing hatchet job, a weary Terry sighed and said no. It was about black women bonding and sharing common experiences and problems.

The problem with that was that the publisher didn't bankroll a big promotional campaign for the book, reviewers didn't go ballistic over it, and many black women didn't buy it to read about women bonding over their professions, careers, work experiences, household affairs, children, racism, politics, or women's rights. The world went crazy over it because it gave black women an open license to vent their hostilities, disappointments, frustrations, fears, and paranoia about men, BLACK MEN. And why not? Terry and the women and men who went into delirium over *Waiting* had a lot of history on their side.

II

From slavery to the present, black men listened to white men savage, twist, malign, libel, batter, and mug them in conversation, books, and the press. It was painful, but at least they understood it. They told themselves that white men feared, envied, and despised them. Or they rationalized it by saying, "It's a man's thing." By this they meant that many white men viewed black men as competitors and potential challengers to their power and control.

But now black women were bad-mouthing them, too. Books. TV talk shows. Newspaper articles. Movies. Everywhere they turned black women were talking about them. The things they said about them sounded suspiciously like the same things many white men said about them.

Note: For a hot minute some black men got perverse revenge with Shahrazad Ali's The Blackman's Guide to Understanding the Blackwoman (1989). *Ali dogged black women. She called them bossy, pushy, domineering, gold diggers, gossips, backbiters, whiners, disrespectful, and sex connivers. Some black men had a hearty laugh when Ali said black women were lousy housekeepers, unkempt, and wore dirty braids. It didn't last. She and the men that giddily embraced Ali's* Guide *as their guide were fighting at best a rearguard holding action. The women were determined to have their say—about men.*[2]

Michele Wallace launched the attack in the early 1970s with her book *Black Macho and the Myth of the Superwoman.* Wallace claimed that black men's obsession with white women bordered on the clinical. The woman took special delight in downing the men of the Black Power movement. To her, they were a bunch of phonies that used the movement as a cover to satisfy their lust for white women.[3]

What could you say to this? She gave no figures or data on interracial marriage, dating patterns, or even bed hopping to back this up. It was one woman's bitter opinion, nothing more. Black men panting after white women. It got a lot of play.

Then there was Ntozake Shange's *For Colored Girls*. Shange introduced us to Willie Beau. He was an irresponsible, loathsome drunk who pisses on himself and wallows in his vomit. He hates his woman (and himself) so much that he throws his own kids out the window.[4]

During the 1980s, the "new era" black women writers stepped up the attack. They styled themselves as tough, no-bullshit, take-no-prisoner sisters ready to smash "the code of silence" about sexism and tell the raw truth about black men.

They wrote books. Gloria Naylor's *The Women of Brewster Place* introduced four black women. Not one had a real man. They had to suffer through guys who were mostly liars, unstable egomaniacs, dick grabbers, pussy chasers, and gang rapists. One woman doggedly tried to make a go of it with her man. For her efforts, she was ignored, cursed out, and whacked. When he finally decides to walk out, she begs him to stay, pleading, "I love you." He rewards her devotion by gruffly telling her, "Well, that ain't good enough." BAM.[5]

Alice Walker's *The Color Purple* finally drove some black men to revolt. Alice named her black man simply "Mister." "Mister" was anyman. He was a misogynist, tyrant, abuser, child beater, and wife batterer. Even though he saw the light and became a better man at the end of the story, the damage had been done. "Mister" would be remembered as a brute.

Black men cried foul and accused Walker of savaging them. "E.T." Spielberg didn't care one way or another that Hollywood never seemed to find a black man who didn't shoot, beat, drink, snort, or screw his way across the screen; *The Color Purple* sounded like a good yarn to him. And since E.T. had made a bundle turning yarns into juvenile other world fantasies, *The Color Purple* became the smash movie hit of the year. Even though Walker later claimed that she got the short end of the money stick from the film, she still stuck to her guns and said the film was still pretty much on target about black men.[6]

Black men groused even more. But this was so much sour grapes. Many black women rallied to the women's defense. They told the men to quit bellyaching and change the reality. They felt duty-bound to defend Walker, Shange, and Naylor when they were perceived as being under attack by black men for creating demeaning images.[7]

Note: I was one of their critics. I never attacked them for creating demeaning images of black men. I attacked them for creating no other kind of image. We can all name countless numbers of black men whose lives embody positive images. They don't have to be created.

III

Still, trying to "change the reality" is a tall order, particularly since many black feminists are convinced that black men like their white brethren gorge themselves at the trough of "patriarchy." Some black feminist theorists dug deep into history to "prove" that black men were sexist before slavery. Presumably they referred to male-female relations within African society before the European conquest. The popular notion is that the men had many wives. The women cooked, cleaned, took care of the kids, and served the men. Nothing more.[8]

They made two mistakes. They judged African communal society by Western standards. African communal society was not European industrial society. In feudal Europe, a woman was bound by tradition and rights to the baronial estates. She was both economic producer and care giver. Her labor was vital to the economic life of the clan or village. The European industrial revolution changed this. The power of the industrial bourgeoisie was based on the iron-clad rule of private property, commodity production, unfettered profit, and personal possessions. The historic customs, traditions, and duties of women were obliterated. The marriage contract resembled a property contract. A woman became a personal possession. Her labor and service were bound to one man in one home. In the factory, capitalist dominance became supreme. In the home, male dominance became supreme.[9]

In African communal society, private property and commodity production for profit were alien. Women were not commodities or property objects. They were not bound by a formal contract to serve and perform labor for one man. They were a vital part of the economic and social life of the village or clan. The household was organized to facilitate shared responsibilities for food production, trade, and goods management. Women's roles were respected and honored.

Their second mistake. Polygamy is much criticized and much misunderstood. Not all West African societies were polygamous. A sizable number didn't practice it at all. In those that did, men did not simply collect and subjugate women for sex, personal gratification, and child breeding. The system evolved mostly out of economic and social necessity. Men had a nasty tendency to get themselves killed in wars, accidents, or while hunting.

In a communal society organized on the basis of economic sharing and mutual protection and defense, a bride was integrated into the economic and social life of the male household. There was no "contract." She did not serve him. She served the group. Child care was a shared responsibility.

Ashanti fathers and mothers had equal responsibility for the care, nurturing, and raising of their children. There was far more flexibility in gender relations and in the interchange of work. These were fewer stigmas attached than previously thought to men doing so-called women's work and women doing so-called men's work.[10]

Slavery temporarily blurred the gender lines. Black men and women were brutalized, dehumanized, stripped of their culture and language. Black men and women were physically, economically, and legally powerless to form, build, nurture, and defend their families or develop permanent social relationships. The slave master was THE only man on the plantation.

They argued that emancipation changed this. They claimed that black men were in a mad dash to defend male patriarchy, and the black family quickly mirrored the white family. Black men worked, paid the bills, and made the decisions. Black women raised the kids, did the housework, and followed orders. If black women stepped out of line, they were abused or beaten. Sex was the clincher. Black men, like white men, turned the black women into a sex slave while they were free to roam.

But there was much evidence that the gender roles in black homes were always more fluid than in white households. Black women worked, and many black men did share in the housework. Black fathers were more involved in nurturing and raising their children than white fathers. Black men and women overwhelmingly agreed that black men were just as likely to be sharers, givers, and takers in that order as black women were.[11]

Then there is the eternal problem of sex, sex, sex. Some black and white feminists take it to the outer limits and claim that patriarchy makes husbands and lovers rapists in disguise.[12]

Put another way, it's impossible for a black man and woman to build a sensitive, caring relationship based on love and mutual respect. Sex will always get in the way and dirty things up. Well, when you construct a straw man argument, no matter how silly or ridiculous it sounds, you can't lose. But happily, this kind of madcap thinking is so way out that most reputable feminists disavow it. They know that this is the kind of silliness that gives their enemies plenty of ammunition to denounce, discredit, and dismiss the entire women's movement as a bunch of feminazis.

IV

By the 1990s, the attack on black men had turned into a rout. Black women complained bitterly on TV talk shows, in books, and in magazine articles that they couldn't find "Mr. Right." They were getting more frustrated by the day. Many black women longed for someone to tell the world once and for all about the misery and heartache these louses were causing them. They wanted someone to show them how to exhale again.

So Terry did. She and Hollywood transformed the book *Wait-*

ing to Exhale into the movie. While it lost something in the translation, the same cast of characters—Gloria, Savannah, Bernadine, and Robin—still couldn't find a good man among the sad-sack dysfunctional bunch of deadbeats, misfits, drug addicts, alcoholics, and insensitive brutes they met. The familiar stereotypes of black men from the past century came crashing together with a vengeance in their lives. The men all slobbered over white women (lustful brutes). They were all ready to hit the road at the first sign that the women wanted them to make a commitment (irresponsible, unstable). They wouldn't know how to tell the truth even under penalty of death (conniving, calculating, and deceitful). They are lazy, slothful, and will pick a sister's purse or her pants in a minute (immoral, derelict).

Note: There is one additional functional relationship in the book but not in the film, that of a couple married thirty-nine years. By the time we meet them, the man is an old broken-down mule dying of Alzheimer's disease. His wife does everything for him. The message: the only time a black man needs a black woman is when he's helpless, ready to be put out to pasture, and can't find any other skirt (presumably white) to chase.[13]

Many black women went wild over this stuff, not because it "was only fiction" as some women snapped, but because they believed it was fact. They were *those* women in the book and the film. Gloria spoke for them when she bitterly complained that "all men cause pain." It was like peeping in on the pages of *True Confessions.* If *Waiting,* the book, was confirmation for many black women of all the male rot in their lives, the film was their liberation. They rolled up in limos. They whooped, howled, and shouted back at the screen. Many danced, strutted, and paraded triumphantly out of the theaters. They joyously raised champagne toasts in the parking lots. They planned *Waiting* seminars, retreats, cruises, and symposiums. The cash registers jingled madly in Hollywood.

Note: The women that I heard rave the most about the book and the film were college-educated, professional, middle-class black women. Were the men in Waiting *the only kind of men they could find with whom they could have relations? If so, what does that say about them? Worse, what did it say about the women in* Waiting *who at times seemed more preoccupied with the size of a guy's penis than his brains?*

Even Terry said enough was enough and warned that some women were going way off the deep end and not getting her true message: that women can also be slothful and roguish in life and love and need to take responsibility for their actions.

Some critics weren't impressed by *Waiting* and panned it as light fluff. But they were in the minority. Most loved it. They declared it a smash success. As I read the reviews and listened to the talk, a little voice kept whispering something in my ear that an old Black Muslim brother told me years ago: "If he's for it, beware." The he to him was the "white devil." To me it's the corporate-controlled media.[14]

The media has a huge impact in shaping the attitudes of many Americans toward black men and black women. If many Americans see black men and women honestly trying to grapple with and bridge the gender divide, then this is healthy. If instead they accept Hollywood's vision and see black men and women as locked in a hate-filled, sex-driven dance of degradation and dysfunctionality, then the shop-worn stereotypes about both black men and women are reinforced in the collective mind of America (and the world).

My worst fears were quickly confirmed. In the middle of an interview on black parenting I did with a radio station in a small Oregon town, the host suddenly asked me, "Why can't black men get along with their women?" Huh? How did he know that? This guy lived in a town that hadn't seen a black since the Johnstown flood, yet this Peeping Tom was snooping into our collective bedrooms and thinking he knew everything about blacks.

Look, rabbis are appalled at the low number of Jewish women

marrying Jewish men. Would the radio host ask them why they can't get along with each other? Writers Amy Tan and Isabel Allende blister Chinese and Latino men repeatedly for their domineering, macho abuse of Chinese and Latina women. Would he ask them why they can't get along with each other? Many Korean men have been compelled to go to violence-prevention workshops in Los Angeles because they beat and physically abuse their wives. Would he ask them why they can't get along with each other?[15]

For more than a century, white feminists have been denouncing white men for chauvinism. Would he ask himself why he can't get along with his woman? But, this small-town yokel had no compunction about asking that about black men and women.

Maybe I was reading too much into all this. So I asked a friend who read *Waiting* why she liked it. She said softly, but firmly, "She spoke for the hurt of every woman who got dressed up, ready for a date, and the guy didn't show." I asked her the same question about the film. She reiterated: "That's the way many men treat women." The consolation was that she had grown enough in the years between reading the book and viewing the film to add the powerful qualifier "many" before men.

Both times I resisted mightily the urge to shoot back, "You're right, but I do remember the pain I felt when I spent a day washing and polishing my car, getting dressed up, buying flowers, and going to pick up my date only to be met at the door by her sister, who embarrassedly told me that she had just left."

That would have been schoolyard one-upsmanship. It would have been tantamount to my telling a Native American that life is rougher in the ghetto than on the reservation. I held my tongue, cut my losses, and cooled it, secure in the knowledge that I was a man. And as we all know, of course, black men can never have relationships that cause them pain. I did, however, decide to write new love scenarios for the women of *Waiting*. Here they are.

Robin's boyfriend does not take her to meet his dope-dealing friends, and later, steal her purse. He takes her to a church social. Afterwards, they have dinner at a restaurant at his expense.

Bernadine's husband doesn't skip off with his pretty young white secretary. They are still happily married.

The "jerk" that Savannah gets to drive her from Denver to Phoenix does not "make a monstrous face" or "wild beast-like sounds" while banging her hard at the motel where they stop for the night. In fact, they don't jump in the sack at all. They spend several hours relaxing at a nearby club, talking about each other's lives and their future plans. Later, when he calls and asks her if he can come to her room, she says she's tired. He softly wishes her good night.

Gloria's teenage son, Tarik, doesn't pick girls "who looked white" to date. Instead, he has a steady girlfriend who *is* dark-skinned and wears a natural hairstyle.

The older married couple talk exclusively about the years together before he became sick. If we listen closely to them, we might discover some real truths about how to maintain a lasting relationship.

Note: *Even Terry might agree that many blacks need different endings to their lives and loves. She pleaded for women not to exclude their boyfriends, husbands, ex-husbands, lovers, or just any man they care about from the* Waiting *champagne parties. She understood that it's far easier for women to savage men than try to understand them.*[16]

Don't yawn. If we honestly think about it, there are many Savannahs, Bernadines, Robins, and Glorias in relationships with black men who aren't afraid of commitments, nurture their children, value companionship, and want romance with a black woman. I have to specify black woman, since the women of *Waiting*, think that black men only want those kinds of relations with white women. That's not so.

Ninety-five percent of black men marry black women. Most of the guys that marry white women don't do it because they think these women are goddesses, forbidden fruit, or possess mythical status. Nor do they marry them because they are lustful or filled with self-hate. They marry them for the same reason black men marry black women. They share common interests, and they love them. If they didn't, and they tried to build a relationship on sex thrills, fads, or infatuation and not real feeling, it would be like building a house on quicksand. It would sink fast.[17]

A Double Note: (1) Interestingly, the black women who habitually say that their personal relationships are rotten are not middle-income, professional women like Savannah, Bernadine, Robin, and Gloria. They are lower-income, less-educated black women. Now if just one of the legion of sociologists who make careers out of studying Negroes would ask lower-income, less-educated white women about their relationships, I wonder what they'd say?

(2) Every black woman worried sick that ALL black men want white women should take this test. Think of all the black men you know. Now how many of them exclusively pursue, date, are married to, or spend every waking moment chattering about white women? Don't cheat.

V

A final question. Is there a major New York publisher willing to spend bundles of money to advertise and promote a book about a black man who cooks and serves dinner to his family, dons an apron and does dishes, and reads a bedtime story to his son or daughter? My publisher at Middle Passage Press thought so. These are the black men I talk to, and about, in *Black Fatherhood: The Guide to Male Parenting*. Soon after the book was released, my publisher called me excitedly and said that she had just received a call from a major mass-market paperback publisher in *New York*. The company told her they were interested in obtaining reprint rights for the book.[18]

From the type of books I see churned out these days on black male-female relationships, I knew most major publishers weren't interested in publishing books about black men who work hard to build positive, meaningful relationships with their children, wives, and significant others without drugs, alcohol, crime, gangs, violence, and abuse. Even if they are, they still wouldn't publish them because they don't believe the reading public would spend a penny to read them.

But she was so excited that I didn't want to say anything to muck up her mood. Weeks went by with no word from the publisher. She wrote letters and made calls. Finally, they told her sorry, no go.

I still didn't say anything. I thought of the men and women that loved sister Terry's book and the film. Then I really knew why. It finally gave them the chance to exhale. They were exhaling black men.

Chapter 10

No Thriller for Michael Jackson

I'm pretty sure that Michael Jackson learned his lesson. His wealth, success, fame, Casper-the-ghost-looking bleached skin, nose-pinch job, eye shadow, straight hair, and gyrating hips didn't erase two words on his birth certificate: *black male*. He may have forgotten this for a time during his years as a professional entertainer and recluse, but the press didn't. All it took was the unsubstantiated word of a thirteen-year-old that Mike was a child molester and sex abuser to slap him back to reality. The press pounced on him like vultures picking over carrion. The charge was sexual molestation. For a black man who makes his living grabbing his crotch before millions, he was done in from the start. The equation looks like this: black man + sex + perversion = guilt.[1]

Jackson and other black men who wind up on the sexual hot seat remind me of the luckless Americans during the McCarthyite purges of the 1950s. Their personal lives were picked apart by congressional inquisitors. They were battered in the press. Their careers and reputations were destroyed. To escape the shame, some fled the country; others committed suicide. All it took was the unsubstantiated charge that they were Communists or "fellow travelers" or knew someone who was.

It made no difference whether the charge was true. The witch hunters howled for blood. Politicians, the press, and the public tried, convicted and condemned the accused. Years later, a lucky few would be vindicated. Some even resumed their careers. But, the damage had been done. The stigma could never be erased.

We look back on those disgraceful years and swear to the high heavens that it could never happen again in America. But it can. Today, being called a Communist may bring laughter; being called a child or sex abuser, however, will damage a career. It began with the child abuse revelations in the McMartin preschool case. It gathered steam with the sex-abuse charges leveled at Clarence Thomas by Anita Hill. It came full blast when Michael Jackson was accused of both.

Note: In a cover story a year after the Jackson controversy, U.S. News & World Report finally got around to asking "Sexual Predators: Can They Be Stopped?" All the pictures on the cover and inside were of white males. But where were their features and stories when the press relentlessly slammed Jackson? This might have helped counter the public perception that men like Jackson were America's sole child sexual abuse culprits.[2]

The media quickly displayed its magnificent talent for turning trivia and gossip about Jackson into the "big story." So what if the police didn't find anything? So what if no one bothered to do a background check on the accuser and the alleged witnesses? So what if the district attorney did not immediately press criminal charges? So what if no one cared how many luggage bags Liz Taylor carried on the plane when she went to meet Jackson on his world concert tour?

The media happily titillated the public with countless "in-

sider" interviews, features, and reports on Jackson's alleged she-
nanigans. It worked. Based on an unsubstantiated charge, the
press got the tongues of the public wagging.

II

I suppose it was only a matter of time before Jackson wound up
in the dock. He was always ripe for the pickings. Besides being
incredibly rich, he's also obsessively reclusive. The press easily
turned the privacy he spent a lifetime guarding into a damning
weapon against him. Even when he bowed to the critics and
tried to show he was a real person by venturing an opinion or
two, his words came back to haunt him.

In 1992, he told *Ebony* magazine, "Children are loving, they
don't gossip, they don't complain, they're just open-hearted,
they're ready for you. They don't judge." Oh, boy! "What did
he *really* mean by that?" asked a critic for the *Nation* turned
amateur psychoanalyst. He seemed giddy at the prospect of dis-
covering something murky and sinister in those stray remarks.
Stuff like this probably made Jackson wish he had kept his trap
shut and stayed hidden on his ranch.[3]

The bewildered Jackson continued his world tour in a vain
effort to keep up the appearance of normality. But the charges
still continued to fly and a lawsuit was filed against him. As
usual, the case boiled down to Jackson's word against his accuser's. His prospects weren't good. Even if Jackson could have
won in a court of law, he would have lost in the court of public
opinion. Jackson knew it. All he wanted was to get on with his
life and career. He chose the better part of valor. He settled with
his accuser for millions.

He then tried every kind of damage control. He cut a new
album (and managed to piss Jewish groups off by rashly and
stupidly using the word "Kike" in the lyrics of one of the songs).
He talked to Barbara (Walters). He resurrected Elvis in daughter
Lisa, married and then divorced her. He talked of another world
tour. He got sick (his enemy sister La Toya claimed he did it to
get sympathy). But people have long memories and even longer

tongues when it comes to the emotionally hypercharged issue of child sexual abuse. The rumors, whispers, and doubts will almost certainly plague him for years.

He isn't alone. Others have suffered the same fate. In 1995, there were more than a million reported child sexual abuse cases nationally. And many thousands more weren't reported. Although only a small percent of the cases resulted in criminal prosecutions, many of the accused still paid a price.[4]

A good friend was one. He was accused of abuse against his stepdaughter. He isn't rich or famous like Jackson, so he was spared the ordeal of a media trial. Still, he was grilled by social workers, the police, and a prosecuting attorney. He spent thousands of dollars on legal fees. He lost days from his work for court appearances. All because of the unsubstantiated charge made by the child's father, who had a bitter grudge against him and his ex-wife. Although the case was dropped due to insufficient evidence, the damage was done. The memory will haunt him forever.

Still, I say with no hesitation that the authorities are duty-bound to flush child sex abusers out of hiding. When the facts clearly warrant it, they must prosecute. The problem is they should have done that all along. My friend, Jackson, and countless other men wind up as suspects because the legal system ignored child and sexual abuse charges or treated them as nuisance cases for years.

Only after feminist and child advocate groups screamed about society's insensitivity did lawmakers and the courts pass and enforce tougher laws. Yet in their mad dash to judgment, they did not develop clear definitions and standards that preserved the rights of both victim and accused. Ultimately, this is the best guarantee that child sex abusers will wind up behind bars and stay there.

Note: Woody Allen is one of my favorite funnymen. I've seen most of his films. But I couldn't help but compare his plight to that of Mike's. Even though Woody was raked over the coals and pilloried with every kind of accusation of kinky and abusive sex with his child/lover/stepdaughter, Woody's film director peers at the Directors Guild didn't hold it against him. They awarded him the prestigious D. W. Griffith award in 1995. We'll see how Mike is honored by his music industry peers in the coming years.[5]

———————

As long as the legal lines are blurred, it will be virtually impossible to prevent opportunists from using child- and sex-abuse laws for revenge or personal gain. This gives the press free license to run amok and peddle gossip as fact. Jackson is tragic proof that public witch hunts damage reputations but do not educate the public about the very serious problem of child sexual abuse.[6]

Maybe that's why a perplexed Jackson shook his head and mumbled, "But I love children, I always have." Until a judge or a jury tells me otherwise, I believe him. That's the American way —at least on paper.

Chapter 11

What's Love Got to Do With It? More Than You Think

I wonder how many people bothered to read pages 206–207 in Tina Turner's autobiography, *I, Tina*. She doesn't mess around. In three words, she said what she really thought about men. "I love men." There were no ifs, ands, or buts. If ever a woman was entitled to ifs, ands, and buts, it's Tina. Many of us know her story.[1]

For nearly two decades Ike and Tina Turner were hot-ticket items. There was Tina gyrating wildly on stage belting out hard-driving rhythm-and-blues numbers in that peculiar guttural voice of hers. They were the real deal. You could look at them and practically smell the collard greens, cornbread, and ham hocks. You knew they had paid hard dues in some of the raunchiest dives around before they made it to the big time.

What we didn't know was that behind the scenes Tina caught hell. She was tormented by a possessive, paranoid, coke-addicted bully. Ike beat her with fists, belts, iron cords, hangers, and boots to keep her in line. Much of this was shown in the movie about her life. Many certainly walked out of the theater shaking their heads and thinking, "Yeah, what would you expect. That's the way those black guys treat their women."

Tina didn't see it that way. She did not wring her hands, weep and wail about being a battered woman. She was not going to be a symbol, a martyr, or a marionette for the cause of feminism. She made no apologies for her years with Ike. She didn't sharpen her knives on Ike's or other black men's hides. She was not a fool in love. Tina had words for the "intellectuals" (her word, not mine) who tried to tell her she was. "I don't give a crap what they think. I did what I had to do there."[2]

She had no regrets at giving Ike manicures, pedicures, choosing his clothes, changing his hair style, being there at his beck and call, and catering to his every whim and mood. Even if she had been awake for hours, she didn't get out of bed until he did. She did these things not because he wanted it, but because she wanted it. As far as she was concerned Ike was one man, not *all* black men. "Although I had a bad relationship, it did not change my feelings about men."[3]

What are those feelings? Let's start with her father. There is only scant mention of him in the movie. But in her book she talks a lot about him. After her mother skipped off, she and her sister lived with him for five years.

Note: *The movie gave the impression she lived only with her grandmother.*

————————

Tina says he was a man who was a hard worker. He kept his daughters in food and clothes. He bought a bigger house for them. Eventually, he ran off, too. Tina doesn't say why. Maybe he felt overwhelmed trying to take care of two teenage daughters without a wife. Maybe he was frustrated. Maybe there was another woman. Who knows? Tina hasn't forgotten that he ran off. She was hurt: "I was so mad at my father." This showed that she cared deeply about him. This is her way of acknowledging that he did try. I believe she has forgiven him.

II

Post-Ike. Tina is not afraid to say that she wants her men to be masculine. She wants a man who can stand his ground and be firm. She believes that there are clear gender roles and differences between men and women. Tina revels in them. She measures beauty in part by a man's physical strength. For her this is something a man should be proud of. She doesn't run from those feminine distinctions in herself. She sees strength in being a woman. "I love every oil, every cream, every bottle of perfume, anything made for women." She doesn't put these things down as fetishes conjured up to feed into men's sexual fantasies and egos or to fatten the profits for the male-run fashion and cosmetics makers.

She loves the wigs, the short dresses, and the black knit stockings. The woman exudes sex not as a commodity but as an expression of personal sensuality. She's a woman in control, a woman who knows her mind and her body and is not ashamed of it.

In the years away from Ike, Tina has done a lot of thinking about relationships. She knows what she wants. While she wants her man to be strong and masculine, she also wants him to "respect me and my strengths as a woman." Respect. She wants it. She demands it. She deserves it. She's willing to do the things that are necessary to make a relationship work.

She's willing to be there, be caring, be supportive, be attuned to his needs, be sensitive to his problems. I suspect that she is even willing to go beyond the call of duty for her man. If—*if*—he's willing to respect and appreciate her for that. She's not trying to make him over or recast him. She asks only that he recognize her for what she is and what she has accomplished.

III

In many ways, she reminds me of my mother and the many black women that I knew growing up. They were working-class women, basic sisters, who had a vision of life that included the well-being of their families, their husbands, and themselves. These women were strong, proud women. They did not believe in belittling their men, or putting them down in front of their friends or their children. They did not see themselves in competition with their men. They wanted to work together to make a better life. They didn't feel that they were sacrificing their identity and integrity. They wouldn't have paid that price.

These women were not cowed by their men. They were not afraid to speak their mind and tell them when they thought they were wrong. There were stormy times. Sometimes there was abuse, but they never saw themselves as abused women or victims. They also realized, like Tina, that while some black men were brutal and violent toward their women, many acted this way because of their exaggerated and warped sense of what a man should be and what American society would never allow him to be. Some played out the "bad nigger" role and beat the crap out of black women who had nowhere to go. The laws didn't protect them. Society ignored them. And many in the black community pretended that it wasn't a problem.

Some black men still use their women as punching bags mostly because American society continues to make them its punching bag. There are the daily insults, digs, put-downs, and frustrations. These men are still taught from the crib that it's risky business for a nigger to hit back against whites. In the past, many who did lost their lives or freedom.[4]

But let's be clear: black men have no monopoly on spousal abuse. In a male-dominated society the implicit message men of any color or class receive is that "their women" must be controlled by any means necessary, including by violence. As for black men specifically, nobody claims their brutal actions toward women are right or justified, and certainly no one should dare suggest that they go unpunished, only that there is a reason.

Tina understood. "That's why I stayed. I was in control." If she didn't understand, why else would she have sweated through so many nightmare years with Ike? To me, Tina captures the true beauty, strength, and essence of womanhood. What's love got to do with it? Everything.

Chapter 12

The War on Drugs Is *a War on Black Males*

I wonder why no one listened to William J. Bennett. Here's what the former Reagan drug czar said: "The typical cocaine user is white, male, a high school graduate, employed full-time, and living in a small metropolitan suburb."

Someone might think that Bennett was snorting the white powder himself. Anyone who watches TV or reads the papers can plainly see that the typical drug user is black, male, a high school dropout, unemployed, and hangs out on a squalid ghetto street corner. That's why Chicago judge Thomas Sumner went into shock when someone told him what Bennett said. "Judging by what I see, I would think the numbers would be totally reversed." The judge must have thought, by golly, those aren't the folks who stand in front of me every day in my court.[1]

But Bennett, a true-blue Reagan conservative and the man who never met a multicultural textbook he liked, was dead right. One of America's worst-kept secrets is that the war on drugs is a war on black men. What else could you call it? The 1992 National Household Survey on Drug Abuse revealed that 8.7 million whites used drugs in one month versus 1.6 million blacks.[2]

White high school seniors were far more likely to use drugs

than black high school seniors. Yet they weren't being swept out of suburbia and into prison the way blacks were being swept out of their neighborhoods.[3]

Note: Some blacks who definitely should know better also feed the stereotypes. Colin Powell is an example. During Black History Month, the general was asked to say a few words of encouragement to an honors seminar of three hundred black high schoolers in Los Angeles. He told them simply to "stay in school and stay away from drugs." What made him think that they didn't and wouldn't? These were honor students and high achievers. Why not tell them about college, careers, and academic awards, or praise their parents? Perhaps the general forgot, but I'm sure those were the things that someone must have told him when he was their age.[4]

The police and many politicians say it isn't racism. They claim that more blacks deal the drugs and create a greater menace to their communities. Not true. A few sociologists didn't just watch TV, they actually talked to the people who were using the junk. They found that white male users (93 percent) were way more likely to sell drugs than black male users (67 percent). White males also started using heroin at a much younger age than black males and continued to use it longer.[5]

It shouldn't be hard to figure out why. They have the money and the connections. They know the suppliers. They do not live in the ghettos. They are less likely to be arrested. In candid moments some police officials admit they bust more blacks than whites. It's easier. They're all over the streets, oodles of them. They might as well have a sign hanging on them: "Arrest me." It's numbers man, just numbers! The whites? Many are inside the cozy confines of suburban apartments or high-rise offices.

Note: What would the public think if the police every night took a live TV action camera crew with them and knocked down those suburban doors?

Think about the time, effort, personnel, and resources it takes to find, surveil, and build an airtight case against the big boys. Even when they nail them, they may not make the charges stick. Well-connected dealers know how to twist the law, and if they don't they'll find lawyers who do.

If they succeed in getting white dealers off the streets there's no guarantee the public will know about it. The director of the Massachusetts Division of Alcohol and Drug Rehabilitation confessed that when whites are busted the police are respectful of the families' wishes about "bad" publicity. They are more than happy to help them keep their problems out of the press. I'd add this: the press probably wouldn't care anyway unless the white person busted happened to be named Madonna, Ronald Reagan, or Bill Clinton.[6]

The image of young blacks prone on the ground, handcuffed against walls and over the hoods of police cars makes better copy anyway. TV can get its action photos for the nightly news. The dailies can recycle their customary drug-hysteria-in-the-ghetto story. Police can keep their arrest numbers up. Politicians can prattle about tougher laws. Suburban whites (including the white dope dealers) can breathe a little easier, falsely believing that somebody is really doing something about the problem.[7]

Back in black communities it's business as usual. The number of poor folks who use the stuff or the petty crooks who deal in it grow bigger and more desperate, while the blacks who are their victims still walk in fear.

Note: Despite the press scare stories on "ghetto drug violence" most of the victims are not two-year-old babies, or eighty-year-old grandmothers but the dealers and the users themselves. The murders usually stem from busted drug deals, competition for markets, and disputes over turf.[8]

II

The first press scare stories on drug-crazed black males appeared in the early 1900s. Newspapers fed white fears with bizarre accounts of the criminal exploits of black "cocaine fiends" supposedly on the prowl for white (women) victims. In 1910, Hamilton Wright, reputedly the State Department's then-foremost expert on drug abuse, put the government seal of approval on the fright tales when he testified, "Cocaine is often the direct incentive to the crime of rape by the Negroes of the South and other sections of the country." Wright was way ahead of himself. Three years later Georgia state officials released a study conducted at a Georgia state sanitarium. The officials surveyed more than two thousand black patients and found three drug addicts. Among the whites there were 142 addicts. The numbers of black and white patients were roughly equal.[9]

Between the World Wars, blacks trekked to the North in big numbers to escape poverty, peonage, segregation, and terror. They found no promised land. The North transformed the mostly poor, underemployed, and unemployed Southern black men into mostly poor, underemployed, and unemployed Northern black men. As more blacks sank deeper into the morass of poverty, alienation, and hopelessness, the number of junkies slowly grew.

The big jump came in the 1980s. The Reagan-Bush assault on job, income, and social service programs, a crumbling educational system, and corporate shrinkage dumped more black males on the streets with nowhere to go. Some chose guns, gangs, crime, and drugs. That some was enough. The media quickly got wind of the story and played it big. *Voila!* The drug problem, which is an American problem, now became a black problem.

The public freaked. A majority of Americans were ready to dump constitutional guarantees of due process and privacy. The consequences came with breakneck speed in the form of drug sweeps, random vehicle checks, illegal searches and seizures, and evictions from housing projects and apartments. In the ghetto, many civil liberties protections weren't worth the paper they were written on.

Note: Drug experts estimate that black gangs control only a small percentage of the drug trade. Most of the dope dealers in

black communities are small-time, freelance operators out to
make a fast buck or to support their own habit. The supplies
are tightly controlled by drug cartels. The men who pull the
strings on import, supply, price protection, and contract hits live
far from the borders of these neighborhoods.[10]

III

Between 1986 and 1991, the dope flowed in *both* the ghettos
and the suburbs. The number of whites in state prisons on drug
charges jumped from sixteen thousand to thirty thousand. The
number of blacks in state prisons on drug charges soared from
sixty-five thousand to eighty thousand. Why were so many in
prison? Reagan, Bush, Clinton, senators, and congressmen
watched TV and read the papers, too. From Butte to Peoria, the
public demanded action and the politicians were ready to oblige.
Congress passed legislation imposing mandatory sentences for
all drug-related offenses.[11]

Judges and a few prosecutors balked. They said the government was overreacting and trying to take the legal action from
them. Despite a Mt. Everest-sized stack of documents, studies,
reports, and news features that proved beyond a shadow of a
doubt there was a massive and deep disparity in how black and
white dopers were being sentenced by the feds, the law stood.
Predictably, the number of blacks receiving mandatory federal
sentences quickly rose from a trickle to a flood. The sentences
ranged from ten years to life.[12]

It didn't matter what the circumstances were or how few
grams of white powder were involved. If convicted, that's what
an offender got. One of them was twenty-year-old Michael Winrow. He was convicted in 1989 in Los Angeles for selling five
and one-half ounces of cocaine worth about one hundred dollars
on the street. Winrow got a life sentence. The case caused a mild
stir at the time. Since then, there have been other Winrows and
the public has barely stifled a yawn at their predicament. I do
not, nor should any sane person, condone what men like Winrow do. Even Winrow didn't condone it. When asked, he

shrugged and said all he wanted was a job. Even if he had a job, and was as pious as a monk, he still could have been detained or at least suspected of drug dealing.[13]

Note: Perhaps Winrow's problem was that he didn't know the USC fight song. Two USC seniors did. Both were white frat boys, political conservatives, excellent athletes, and came from sterling middle-class families. Before both OD'd on heroin. neither did any jailtime. In a press postmortem they were painted as innocents. It claimed they bought the drugs in a nearby "drug and crime-infested" neighborhood and were inexperienced users. They weren't. They had used the stuff repeatedly. Friends knew about it. One was hospitalized after an earlier overdose (which meant the authorities knew about it). The writer did not present a shred of evidence that they bought the dope in the hood. In fact, most drugs are sold by and bought from friends, relatives, or acquaintances. These men committed crimes. They were no less culpable than the Winrows of the world, yet the press treated it as a tragic human interest story and not once mentioned the words "crime" and "punishment."[14]

————

With the media fanning the flames, black men everywhere, job or no job, profession or no profession, Ph.D. or no Ph.D. suddenly found themselves stopped at roadblocks, shaken down on city streets, questioned in department stores and having makes run on them. This was especially galling for members of the new black bourgeoisie. No matter how far their money or status took them from the "hood," much of white America still saw them as hoods.[15]

An example: Joe Morgan was casually chatting on the phone at the Los Angeles airport between flights. Next, Joe found himself body-slammed to the floor and tussling with two white undercover cops. They claimed that Morgan fit the Drug Enforcement Administration's "drug courier" profile. Since neither officer was a Cincinnati Reds fan, Mr. Hall of Famer was just another nigger to them. As it turned out, Morgan was a very expensive "nigger." The Los Angeles City Council eventually agreed to pay him $796,000 to settle his lawsuit.[16]

Even though black professionals like Morgan protested, threatened, and even won lawsuits, police and prosecutors shot back that this was a war and sometimes innocents get hurt. Nobody, however, saw middle-class white executives or professionals in crucifixion-like stances against walls, or leaning with their hands stretched out over the hoods of their expensive Porsches and Benzes.

What about the white dopers? Many of them were shunted to state court where judges still had some say over sentencing. They received less time (if any) in state prison. In New York, state courts extended their *noblesse oblige* to cocaine dealers while stigmatizing crack dealers. Cocaine dealers were more likely to be released on their own recognizance or low bail and receive a shorter sentence (remember the four "P's"—press, public, panic, and perceived danger) than crack dealers. You get one guess who the majority of crack dealers were in the eyes of the law.[17]

The cruelest joke of all is that none of this has amounted to a hill of beans in the drug war. Federal and state officials have squandered billions of dollars locking up mostly poor black and Latino males (and increasingly black females). Yet the junk still floods the ghettos, barrios, and suburbs. Federal officials desperately search for a winning strategy. It will be tough. By allowing the media to create the fiction that the drug problem is a black problem, they've dug themselves into a deep hole.

The GOP said no in 1995 to any increase in drug treatment funds and rehabilitation programs. They are politicians and they know that there is no real public consensus for spending massive funds on drug treatment and rehabilitation programs. Police and prosecutors know the huge legal battles they'd have to wage in making the fat-cat dealers their prime targets. Most Americans damn sure won't seriously debate the legalizing of some drugs to cut crime. And politicians damn sure haven't seriously tried to loosen the stranglehold the National Rifle Association uses on Congress to torpedo legislation that might slow down the virtual open trafficking of guns in the ghettos and suburbs.[18]

So people wonder what's next. My answer: watch TV, read the papers, and see who still appears in those flattering police poses.

Chapter 13

The Other Boyz N the Hood

I never understood why so many blacks loved *Boyz N the Hood*. But they did. Friends, acquaintances, and even relatives went nuts over it. Even some who prided themselves on being political sophisticates and who should have known better tossed sanity out the window and heaped praise on the film for telling the raw truth about the ghetto. After a while it got so bad that I stopped arguing with people about the film.

But I had to give it to the filmmaker. He did what an army of psychologists, sociologists, historians, and government bureaucrats couldn't do. He managed to convince Bill Clinton, many whites, and far too many blacks that the "gangsta" lifestyle was the black lifestyle. It was all there in *Boyz*. Young brothers dissed sisters as "bitches" and "hos," called each other "niggers" and "bitch," cussed, fought and shot at each other. Many patrons left the theaters with smirks on their face as they happily told friends, "Ah, we knew all the time that they were like that." We have seen the enemy and it ain't us.

The minute I dared suggest that the film presented a parade of one-dimensional pop ghetto stereotypes, I was shouted down. Even though I have lived and worked in Watts and South Central Los Angeles for more than thirty years, before many of my critics were even born, they still told me, "You just don't know how it is with blacks." I hadn't seen blacks get so steamed over an issue since Thomas vs. Hill. Finally, I decided to follow the filmmaker's advice and keep the peace. I shut up.

II

Yet I wondered: were blacks that starved to see themselves on the screen that they accepted uncritically the young black film-makers/Hollywood vision of how young black men behaved? A few trotted out the tired line, "Well, we really don't see ourselves that much on the screen." Baloney! For the past five decades, blacks have sung, danced, postured, swaggered, beat, shot, stabbed, and made love to whites on the screen.

They have played cops, robbers, dope pushers, pimps, whores, presidents, corporate heads, astronauts, aliens, devils, zombies, spacemen, and every role in between. They've done everything anybody could think of in lollipop land. I would think that by now they should have been mature enough to discriminate in their movie tastes and demand films that portray them with more dignity than degradation. In short, the thrill of seeing a black face on the screen should be long gone.

I decided that the black love affair with *Boyz* had less to do with the truth about the hood than their ignorance of the hood. Therefore, I thought it appropriate to administer the following test.

Note: What do past and present Hollywood luminaries Suzanne Somers, Al Pacino, and Jane Fonda have in common besides Hollywood? In their youthful days they were all arrested and charged with serious crimes. In fact, at least five hundred celebrities were also arrested and charged with crimes, some serious. Most, like Fonda, Somers, and Pacino, were never prosecuted. The public generally didn't know about their crimes. The me-

dia didn't make a big deal out it. Their careers didn't suffer. Then again, why should I be surprised? Hollywood is not the hood.[1]

III

True or false: most young black males are high school dropouts and low academic achievers?

They aren't. In 1992, nearly 80 percent of African Americans graduated from high school and nearly 30 percent were enrolled in college (many in historically black colleges). Many young blacks have even crashed the doors and strolled in the stuffy halls of elite private academies. At last count, people of color made up about one-fourth of the enrollment at some of these schools. In 1994, four young black men were awarded Rhodes Scholarships. The same year 300,000 young blacks competed in the National NAACP Academic Decathlon. About half of the contestants were males.[2]

Most young black males have higher educational aspirations than young whites. They desire more prestigious positions in business and the professions. This is why, from slavery to freedom, generations of black parents have chanted this mantra to their sons: "Get an education, boy. Get an education, boy. Get an education, boy."

They knew that they had to be two and three times better than whites just to be considered equal (sort of). They've drilled this into their kids' heads and it stuck. Polls always show the same thing. Blacks consider nothing more precious than education.[3]

The bad news is that black males who desperately want degrees are losing ground. Funding cuts, the elimination of scholarships, grants, and financial assistance, during the Reagan-Bush years decimated the ranks of young black males in colleges. Those fortunate enough to get their degrees will make much less than white male college graduates. Young black males haven't given up the dream, but it has become tattered.[4]

IV

True or false: only a small percentage of young black males join gangs.

Even Daryl Gates got this one right. The former embattled Los Angeles Police Department chief, who called the Rodney King beating an "aberration," said that Los Angeles district attorney Ira Reiner went way over the cliff in 1992 when he claimed that half of all young black males in Los Angeles were gang members. Reiner put the number at 150,000. The "chief" squirmed at the figure not because it made the black community look bad but because it made his department look bad.

Others also took Reiner to task for "overstating" the numbers. It was no overstatement. A cynic might say that Reiner, locked in a tight race for reelection, waved the report to the media to get panicky white votes. (He quit before he got beat.) Even if there were no hidden political agenda, the methods used to compile the numbers stank. Many names were counted several times in the database.[5]

Many of the kids whose names wound up in the database wouldn't know the Crips gang from *Our Gang*. Their names were there because police were more interested in colored skins than colored scarves. Jaywalking, pitching pennies, or stargazing, it didn't matter what the pretext; if a young black male was stopped, his name in perpetuity could read "gang member."

My son's name is probably kicking around somewhere in that computer. He's a twenty-three-year-old undergrad majoring in business at California State University, Dominguez Hills. He's a good student. He minds his own business. He hasn't done drugs, joined a gang, or been arrested. Still the police have run more makes on him than Madonna has lewd pictures in her sex book. When he lived at home and left the house, I sweated worrying about his safety. If you're not a black parent with a son under twenty-five, you wouldn't understand.

Computers should not be blamed for turning young black males into potential police lineup candidates. Politicians like Reiner and the press should be. Scare stories and juggled figures on gangs turn the public's justified fear of crime into unjustified hysteria over black crime. They make whites think that any young black man wearing a funny colored shirt (even some black businessmen wearing ties), baggy pants, and earrings, and listening to rap music is a "gangsta." The fact is, no one really knows how many young black males are really in gangs. Gang experts put the figures much lower than the press, politicians, and the public do.

After subtracting the wannabes and the hangers on from the total, they say that maybe one in five young black males is a hard-core gang member (that's also way too high). We should also consider who the perpetrators and the likely victims of gang violence are. Innocent bystanders are not at the greatest risk. Police officials trace less than one in ten victims of violent crime to gangs.[6]

Note: Can you believe someone actually claimed that the few blacks who do kill and terrorize the hood are smitten by an "urban survival syndrome"? This harebrained sociological gibberish is phony, self-serving, and a badly flawed effort to allow the few real "hoods" to literally get away with murder. Blacks must always distinguish between brotherhood and the brother who's a hood.[7]

The worst ones to ask for numbers are the gang members themselves. Some of the "leaders," drunk with their newfound celebrity status courtesy of appearances on "Geraldo," "Oprah," "Donahue," and "Nightline," wildly exaggerated their importance and power. They've been helped along not only by the press, but by some doting black leaders who hail them as Malcolm X's reincarnated. They forget that Big Red was an avid reader in prison. He studied and debated for many years before he became Malcolm X. If many of the gang "leaders" raised a book, it's an act of God. Only a few scant months before "Nightline"'s Ted Koppel discovered them, many were more concerned with the contents of the pocketbooks of old ladies on the streets of the hood than textbooks.

Some of the older gang-bangers who have paid their dues doing long stretches in joints throughout the nation have had time to think about the "gangsta" lifestyle. Stanley "Tookie" Williams is one. The reputed Crip cofounder is doing hard time at San Quentin. He says it's no mystery why some young black males join gangs. "They feel left out in a white-dominated society." Tookie did not glamorize the life. Listening to him, you just know that men like him are still a distinct minority in the hood and should and will always remain that way.[8]

V

True or false: young black males who join gangs and commit crimes have low self-esteem, are low achievers, and are full of self-hate.

Tookie gave the answer away. But let's elaborate. In 1948 psychologist Dr. Kenneth Clark conducted his famous "doll tests" on groups of black kids. He put the children in a room with black and white dolls and observed the ones with which they played. He found that many of them picked the white dolls. Clark wasn't surprised. This demonstrated that the years of segregation, poverty, and denial had made black kids feel worthless. White is right, black stay way back. Clark hoped that the test results would persuade the Supreme Court to strike down school segregation in *Brown* vs. *Board of Education*.

Sadly, the well-meaning Clark had planted a bad seed. During the 1960s the sociologists reaped the grim harvest. They followed Clark's lead and conducted their own tests on black children. They concluded that the ghetto was a hopeless muddle of poverty and deviancy. Blacks were hapless, self-hating, ambitionless wastrels. Clark blamed racism. Many sociologists and psychologists blamed blacks. A spate of scholarly articles hammered hard on this theme.[9]

By the 1970s, a few researchers became suspicious. There were just too many blacks chasing careers, diplomas, and degrees. Even the ones who weren't said they'd like to if they had the chance. The researchers backtracked to the original Clark tests. With all due respect to the professor, they suggested that he really hadn't proven that blacks hated themselves. He proved only that: a) They did not play with black dolls because they didn't have them. b) They played with white dolls because they were curious about them. c) Even then, a significant number of the kids preferred to play with black dolls. When others duplicated the tests years later and included white kids, they found a sizable number of black and some white children chose the black dolls for play activity.

Note: Since "self-hating white people" is an oxymoron in American society, nobody would dare accuse whites of self-hate or low esteem.

These psychologists blew the old theories apart. They found that many black high schoolers had the same if not greater self-esteem, self-worth, and self-initiative than many whites. Black children were not mesmerized by everything white. They were more concerned about what their friends, parents, and relatives thought about them than what whites did.[10]

If a black child went bad, it wasn't because he thought that he was a miserable wreck of a person. It was because he knew he lived in a miserable wreck of a society that denied him a decent education, job, and hope. A twenty-four-year-old long-time member of the Bloods gang in Watts put it simply: "The average black person I know is just like me and can't get a job. Most of us don't have another way of being somebody other than a gang."

In Los Angeles in 1992, Bloods and Crips gang leaders drew up a peace pact. It contained an elaborate economic blueprint for community improvement. It was hailed by many as a marvel of ingenuity, creativity, and originality. They were not culturally deprived social invalids. The gang truce that they hammered out after the riots held firm for the next two years and the number of gang-related killings in the hood plunged.[11]

VI

True or false: black violence is as natural as apple pie is American.

The truth is that *violence* is as American as Apple pie. *Time* magazine paused briefly from reminding us about the "blood-scarred streets of South Central Los Angeles" (God, why does that sound like something that some eager beaver writer or more likely a grizzled editor remembered from a high school English literature class?) to do a lengthy feature on teen violence in the suburbs. *Time* noted that the FBI found crime and violence inching up in the suburbs while it dropped in the hood. In 1993, more suburbanites than ever said they were cringing at the folks in their own neighborhoods.[12]

Does that mean that there's a subculture of violence germinating in the flowery gardens of suburbia? For years, the media and some sociologists speculated that maybe there's something in the genes, air, or blood of the ghetto poor that makes young black men commit mayhem and murder. This assumes that at heart the black doctor, lawyer, engineer, plumber, or teacher's son is a drive-by shooter or gang-banger. This assumes that racism and poverty are mere trifles and that all blacks have a higher tolerance for violence.

Not true. Young men of all colors commit more crimes and are more violence-prone. How could it be otherwise? They are fed a steady diet of cops, robbers, *Rambo,* and *Terminator* macho violence on TV and in the movies at a time when the testosterone is flowing at record levels in their young bodies. They are taught that fists, knives, and guns (and they're everywhere) rather than discourse, discussion, and compromise are the honorable way to settle disputes. What message does it send about the value of life when young people watch the body count rise while the adults make pious statements about the "senselessness" of the carnage, and then do nothing to stop it?[13]

The "subculture of violence" theorists sometimes point to the astronomically high number of blacks in prisons and jails to prove that young blacks are habitually violent and dangerous.[14]

Not so. In 1991, more than 70 percent of young males arrested were white, 25 percent were black. Yet a strange thing happened between arrest and trial: only 35 percent of whites were held in custody while 44 percent of the blacks were held.

Racism? The experts say no. They claim that they can't lock up their little Johnnies for shoplifting bubble gum, deflating tires, or scrawling "I love Susie" on walls. Juvenile delinquents, yes; criminals, no. They don't peddle dope, gang-rape, shoot babies from moving cars, or rob grandmothers like the "boyz N the hood." But a lot of white "boyz" do these things in their hoods, too.

In 1990, thirty-two thousand more young whites were arrested for murder, forcible rape, robbery, and assault than black juveniles. Even so, three hundred more blacks than whites were placed in custody, and two hundred more blacks than whites were tried as adults. A Chicago probation officer tells how they get away with it. "When children of the middle and upper class do come to court, they often arrive with both parents, community counselors, school representatives bearing report cards, and private attorneys representing them." A poor black kid is lucky if his grandmother shows up in court with him.[15]

Note: In December 1993, the nation was shocked by the brutal strangulation murder of twelve-year-old Polly Klaas. When Richard Allen Davis, a white ex-con, confessed to the murder, more than a few wondered how a guy with nearly twenty prior arrests for crimes that included robbery, assault, possession of a dangerous weapon, and drug dealing could still be out prowling the streets. Two deputies had even stopped Davis within hours of the murder. Davis appeared slightly inebriated, and opened a can of beer and sipped it in front of them. They also found a bag in his car with torn clothes in it. Yet they found nothing suspicious and/or illegal in this. He was released. As always, people blamed the laxity of the criminal justice system. My question: how many black men arrested twenty times for violent crimes or stopped near a crime scene would the system be that "lax" with?

One more thing: Davis apparently wasn't too put out by the national howl to crack down on men like him. His attorney said that he was ready to plead guilty if he could receive life imprisonment rather than the death penalty. No chance. This was one fish that wouldn't get away. He would be tried and convicted. Still, the fact that Davis thought there was yet one more crack he could crawl through should make anyone shudder.[16]

Violence isn't born into young black males. Black males are born into a violent society.

True or false: the culture of poverty breeds violence.

How many dope addicts, dealers, drive-by shooters, carjackers, and muggers do you know that are college graduates, have professions, operate businesses, and are active participants in society's institutions? Now, how many blacks does society deny these educational and economic benefits to? The answer is the same in both cases.[17]

VII

True or false: My wife, Barbara, holds an M.A. degree from the University of Southern California. She is an administrative professional in the university's Real Estate Development Office and a licensed real estate agent. She belongs to several respected civic organizations. She is also a member of the Crips street gang.

I'm not trying to be cutesy. As a lark, if you answered true, you're right. During the course of a staff meeting with other office administrators at her office one afternoon, a white coworker anxiously mentioned that he had spotted some graffiti on a wall near the university's recently completed town-house development. The gentleman wondered if the graffiti was the handiwork of gang members.

While he spoke, Barbara, who happened to be the only black in the meeting, noted that he kept his eyes locked on her. She got the distinct impression he was talking to her. She's not a paranoid person. She generally goes out of her way to give people the benefit of the doubt. She's one of the last persons that whites could accuse of being too sensitive about race or of always seeing racism everywhere. Yet she did think it odd that when the subject was gangs, the whites looked at her. The rest of the time she was mostly ignored.

I mention this only to show the danger of stereotyping. If most whites, nonblacks, and some blacks think that *all, most,* or *the majority* of young black males are gang members, it's only a short and dangerous step for them to assume that indeed *all* blacks wear the colors. That's why the young ex-"gangsta" from Detroit decked out in gold chains and wearing earrings at the gang peace conference in Kansas City in May 1993 had fun with the media. He told news reporters that he thought the conference was bullshit and that he was going to keep on killing.

The fellow walked away with the rest of the reporters tailing him like anxious puppies. Suddenly he turned, laughed, and said that he was lying. One of the more astute reporters couldn't resist. He wrote this about the incident: "He sneered as if to say such a sensational account would have been invented by the media regardless of his true words." He was right.[18]

Chapter 14

Ghetto Chic

I recently watched a popular national TV talk show and heard a noted black author tell a grim tale of abuse, neglect, violence, and poverty during his childhood years. The host and the audience sat in rapt attention. They applauded when he declared that he overcame the "mean" ghetto streets to make something of himself. Supposedly this was a story of hardship and triumph.

Two weeks earlier in two separate talk shows, a prominent black actor and a popular recording artist said that they were raised in a crumbling project or tenement. They did not know their fathers. Their mothers were on welfare. They fought daily battles against drug addicts, rapists, thieves, and murderers. They ran with or away from gangs. They were lucky to be alive. The three stories sounded suspiciously alike. I wondered if I was missing something? Did all blacks grow up poor, destitute, and dysfunctional?

I thought about my childhood years in the 1960s. My parents weren't rich. The neighborhood I lived in was a typical black working-class neighborhood. No one thought of it as a rotting ghetto or broken-down slum. As I remember, most of my friend's parents were in the home. They worked on the railroads, in the factories, at the post office, or as domestics. They made sure their children didn't go hungry and had a roof over their heads. Many of them wore hand-me-down clothes but they weren't ragged and they were always clean. Most of the children managed to finish school.

We were not perennially miserable. We played games, fought, and got into mischief just like white kids. Our neighborhood wasn't crowded with junkies, thieves, rapists, murderers, and drug dealers. There were alcoholics, drug addicts, and violent criminals, but they were a small minority. Most of us had enough sense to steer clear of them and avoid that life.

A female friend remembered much the same about her childhood. She was not molested, raped or sexually abused by a drunken or doped-up father, male relative, or family friend. She knew some women who were, but they were not the majority.

In the 1950s and 1960s, grant-laden sociologists began branding black neighborhoods cesspools of decay. They carved a growth industry out of studying "black deviancy" and "the pathology of the ghetto." In the 1990s a legion of pop scholars put a new twist to ghetto pathology. They didn't just dissect it; they blamed blacks for creating it.

II

I have been accused of being rhapsodic about a bygone past and putting a happy face on ghetto life. "Gangsta" rappers, black novelists, essayists, poets, playwrights, and filmmakers insist that life in today's black communities is a survival test. The reality, they claim, is that people daily dodge bullets, go to funerals of friends and relatives killed by gangs, step over people lying in drug or alcoholic stupors, hide from rapists and molesters, and despair over absentee or abusive fathers. The true reality is that most blacks don't do any of this.

Note: And that includes many of the rappers who make small fortunes pretending that they do. Rappers Snoop Doggy Dog and Tupac ("I am not a gangster") Shakur would testify to that.

In a confessional moment they told interviewers that the lyrics of their gangsta rap didn't depict their life or reality. So why do they do it? M O N E Y = STEREOTYPE = MO' M O N E Y. (Snoop, not me, said he does it for the money.)

By the way, I used the word "testify" knowingly with these guys. Snoop breathed a huge sigh of relief when a jury in Los Angeles acquitted him of murder charges. Tupac whined and pleaded that he was an innocent man when he was sentenced to prison. He was the happiest man on the planet when a judge took mercy on him and granted him an appeal bond. Snoop and Tupac knew that it's one thing to rap and posture about being a gangsta and another thing to actually be imprisoned as one.[1]

Nine out of ten adult black males are not in prison, on parole, or on probation. Nearly eight out of ten young blacks graduate from high school. Nearly six out of ten young blacks reside in two-parent households. Teen pregnancy rates have soared among white girls but sharply dropped among black girls. In California the black teen pregnancy rate is less than half that of white unmarried teens. Three out of four black women have never received welfare payments.

Despite corporate downsizing and the conservative onslaught against affirmative action and spending for job, skills training, and education programs, more than seven out of ten blacks are employed. In the media's favorite "gang and poverty-ridden" projects such as Cabrini-Green in Chicago and Jordan Downs in Watts, there are many non welfare-dependent, two-parent households. The children don't sell drugs, join gangs, get pregnant, or drop-out of school.[2]

But this isn't ghetto chic. Much of the public believes that most blacks are poor, violent, abused, and sexually depraved. The press feeds this stereotype with a daily diet of crime-drugs-gang-dereliction stories and nurtures it with its tabloid obsession with sex, violence, and depravity.

Note: This is a good time spot to clarify something. When I say "public" I'm not just talking about whites, Latinos, and Asians.

*I'm talking about many blacks, too. A lot of them believe the
bunk about themselves. At the Black Expo in Chicago in 1994, I
participated in a panel discussion on the favorite, for-all-seasons
topic, "the crisis of the black family." The moderator, the panelists, and the audience were black. After everyone finished pon-
tificating about how lousy young blacks are, I asked if anyone
knew that several blacks had recently been awarded Rhodes
Scholarships and National Science Achievement Awards, and
that thousands of young blacks had competed in the NAACP
Academic Decathlon that year. Few in the audience had a clue
about this. When I asked them why they didn't know this, they
blamed the "white racist press." Okay. But I also asked why
was much of the black press also deafeningly silent on these
achievements? No one answered.*

Many black personalities have discovered a gold mine in pandering to the profane. They deliberately reassemble their past
into a collection of sordid tall tales. They know that this is a
sure ticket onto sleaze talk shows, brings hefty advances from
publishers, boosts record sales, and secures movie deals. Corporate sponsors and TV producers and corporations cement the
unholy alliance with the ghetto chic crowd by making them a
staple of freaky daytime talk shows. They can count on a horde
of willing young black men and women to mug and shout into
the cameras like trained seals and create spectacles of degradation and displays of dysfunctionality. The panelists and audience
get their fifteen seconds (I wouldn't dignify their antics with
minutes since all are quickly forgotten), and America gets an
Amos-and-Andy, coon-and-minstrel show.

III

The media and black opportunists are not the only culprits.
Black leaders encourage ghetto chic by playing the numbers
game to magnify black misery. They endlessly tell the media
how many blacks are unemployed, in prison, join gangs, peddle

dope, suffer from AIDS, drop out of school, and get pregnant. They depict black life as a vast wasteland of violence and despair and portray black communities in permanent crisis and chaos.

They grab an occasional spot on "Nightline" or "Donahue" and shake a few dollars from the fast-disappearing number of liberals for their pet programs. But the doomsday scenario is not only wearing thin, it is self-defeating. Many Americans believe that the problems of the ghetto are self-made and insoluble. Many politicians agree. They refuse to spend another nickel on job, welfare, health, or education programs, oppose affirmative action, and demand more police and prisons.

Many blacks have become cynical, refuse to support black organizations or causes, circle the wagons in their businesses, professions, or neighborhoods and frantically distance themselves from the black poor.

Some blacks gain from trading in stereotypes about themselves; most lose. And there's nothing chic about that.

Chapter 15

Colin Powell:
An American Journey or
American Dilemma?

I remember the old newsreels of the 1950s that showed millions of Americans singing and chanting "I like Ike." Despite what many hoped, I knew that millions of Americans in 1996 would not be singing and chanting "I like Colin." Colin Powell would not be the Eisenhower of the 1990s. He couldn't win a presidential election. Abraham Lincoln understood the general's first dilemma. "The man who is of neither party, is not—cannot be, of any consequence."[1]

The general was too liberal for the Republican Party. He supports affirmative action, abortion rights, union protections, and gun control, and he opposes welfare scapegoating.

The general was not in the White House. Democrat Bill Clinton is. Although he carries a load of tattered political baggage, he is a well-connected, experienced campaigner. He has the support of his party. He has the prestige of the White House.

The general would have had to run as an independent. Impossible. He had no national organization, campaign strategy, defined political program, or a vision of change for America. He did not have the estimated $40 to $50 million Democrats and Republicans could spend on grants to state parties, phone banks, direct mailings, advertising, and media spots. He did not have access to the $60 million in public funds both parties will get to wage their campaigns. He did not have the $68 million Ross Perot dug out of his deep pockets to self-finance his 1992 campaign.[2]

None of this ever really mattered if the general was simply dangling a presidential bid before the American public as a ploy to sell more books. I never thought the general was that cynical, crass, and mercenary to trump up a fake presidential candidacy to do that. The general, however, certainly had to know that presidential hoopla, even if it was mostly media-contrived, wouldn't hurt book sales. If the general ever really believed that he was the man to right the creaking ship of state, those obstacles would have paled in comparison to his second dilemma—his race. The general knew the problem. In an interview he called racism "exhibit number one" and cited the vile and racist remarks of former LAPD detective Mark Fuhrman in the O.J. trial as evidence that race still matters.[3]

Note: The general didn't pretend that race didn't count. A conservative senator found that out when he slipped, I suppose innocently, and warned one of the general's advisers, "We're going to get your boy." The adviser promptly warned the senator never, and he meant never, to use that word "boy" around the general.[4]

II

But could the general actually have done the impossible and transcended race in the eyes of many whites? On the surface it appeared that he could. Early polls showed that in a head-to-head race with Dole and Clinton, the general could win and that a majority of whites would vote for him. But it was easy for many whites to tell pollsters that. The general indulged the myth that America is a color-blind society. Many whites believe that civil rights laws, court decisions, and affirmative action have expunged racism from America.

They walk into department stores and they see black managers. They turn on the television and see black reporters, commentators, and anchors. They see blacks living next door to them in the suburbs. They live in cities that are run by black mayors and where blacks are a majority on city councils, boards of education, and hold the top police and city department positions.

Judging from his public statements, the general understood that there's an ugly side to racial denial. He was disturbed by the "insensitivity" of Reagan, Bush, and Gingrich to racism. But many whites aren't. They resist programs that benefit minorities and the poor for ostensibly nonracial reasons. They support organizations and leaders that stockpile weapons and rail against federal "tyranny." They elect candidates who promise to cut education, wipe out social programs, permanently kill national health care reform, and build more prisons. Race is never mentioned. It doesn't have to be. Minorities and the poor are hurt the most by this "insensitivity."[5]

Note: The general showed he wasn't afraid to take on one of his bosses, George Bush, for his Willie Horton stunt. The general called the Bush maneuver a "cheap shot." But the general probably also understood the danger of racial stereotyping of black men. He almost certainly recognized that in the minds of many bigots the line between a man like the general and a man like Horton was paper-thin. In fact, many drew no line and the general could just as easily become Willie Powell or Colin Horton.[6]

The general probably knew that in the South no black has won a congressional election since Reconstruction in a nonmajority black voting district. The handful of blacks who have won mayorships with white votes are more political anomalies than trend setters. City councils and city administrators generally control budget and make legislative decisions. While Oklahoma congressman J. C. Watts and Connecticut congressman Gary Frank won office in predominantly white districts, both are staunch

Republican conservatives. They are totally dependent on their party and senior congressional leaders for patronage and political direction. The Presidency, by contrast, is the ultimate visible symbol of national power and decision-making.

For many whites, voting in a straw poll for an African American who is not a declared candidate is risk-free and conscience-salving. The general knew that. CBS commentator Andy Rooney virtually told him so. The windy Rooney thought that a vote for the general was the perfect answer to shut up those blacks who are always screaming racism. The general was having none of it. He made it clear that he was not a black man that closet bigots could wave around to make them feel good about themselves.[7]

If the general had actually chosen to run for President and hit the campaign trail it would have been a different story. He would have been under the most intense scrutiny in American history. He would have been grilled mercilessly by the public and the press on foreign and domestic policy issues. If a skeleton had turned up in Powell's closet, or was placed there, would the press and much of the public presume him innocent and accept his explanations at face value? Or would they have rushed to condemn him? Would the press and his political opponents have used racially loaded code words to attack him?

We'll never know because it never came to that. There were many who weren't awestruck by the general's stars and were determined that he would never get that chance. Pat Buchanan, born-again America's hope for the White House, quickly stepped up to the plate and sternly warned the general that he and his rightist cohorts would make "war" on him if he was really serious about capturing the Republican nomination. "General" Buchanan knew a little something about how to wage political warfare. He hadn't sat around in Nixon's battle rooms for all those years without learning a dirty trick or two that could be used to nail the enemy. The troops quickly lined up behind "General" Buchanan. Their message to General Powell was simple: you don't have the RIGHT stuff for our party and our people.[8]

If the general still wanted to give it a go, they were ready with the one item that was still the general's Achilles' heel: race. They claimed that the general not only championed the hated minority-business set-aside programs (high on the hit list of conservatives) but profited from them to get an ownership share in a Buffalo TV station. They admitted that there was nothing illegal or unethical in the general's business venture. But they knew that this kind of allegation was tailor-made to raise a red flag among those whites hostile to affirmative action. This would force many to question whether an African American in the White House would stick it to whites every chance he got.[9]

If the general had been courageous or foolhardy enough to really try for the Republican nomination, the gloves would have dropped to the floor. "General" Buchanan and the troops would have quickly wiped the mythic public glow from the general. That was the kind of journey that the general was not prepared to take.

Note: The pile of general's books at the flagship Barnes & Noble bookstore in mid-Manhattan resembled a mini Mt. Shasta. Before he announced he would not run, they were flying out the store. The day after he announced he would not run, Barnes removed the pile. Other bookstores in New York and Washington did the same. That ended his other journey.[10]

Chapter 16

The Never-Ending Saga of O. J. Simpson

I got sick of hearing many whites and some blacks hotly deny that race was an issue in the O. J. Simpson case. But then again I could understand why they might think that about the man that an NBC executive described as "the single most popular employee" the network had. He could be called at home any time night or day and would be on a plane for an assignment. When O.J. played for the University of Southern California, it was practically a tradition for USC coaches and recruiters to bring prospective high school recruits over to O.J.'s locker after a game. He was never too tired to greet and encourage them.

In the pros, O.J. never spiked the football. He took his linemen out to dinner to show gratitude for their excellent blocking. Many star National Football League running backs now do the same thing. He often held up the team bus so he could finish signing autographs for the fans. He regularly visited terminally ill children at Buffalo's hospitals, quietly whispering words of cheer and encouragement to them.[1]

He did not become just another burned-out jock when his playing days were over. He crafted a celebrity career as actor, media personality, and businessman. From his earliest days at

USC, O.J. was conscious and protective of his image as a football superstar and personality. He knew that political controversy could diminish his professional market value. Racial controversy might end it.

He made a special point to steer clear of the Black Student Union at USC. When black sprinters Tommie Smith and John Carlos gave their clenched fist black power salute on the victory stand at the 1968 Olympic Games in Mexico City, Simpson was asked his opinion: "I respect Tommie Smith but I don't admire him."[2]

A campus reporter pressed him to give his view of the threatened Olympic boycott by black athletes. O.J. gave what was probably his lengthiest public discourse on sports and black militancy. "I think they're going about the boycott the wrong way. You can't change the world until you change yourself. All this is going to do is make some Negro kid in high school football who isn't playing first string quit, saying, 'This guy isn't treating me right.' " O.J. was the rarest of rare breeds. He was a black man who led a privileged life and was embraced by many whites.[3]

Note: Before O.J. superstar became O.J. accused double murderer there were little danger signs that one slip and fan cheers could quickly change to jeers. When his contract expired in 1973 after his first three years with the Buffalo Bills, O.J. demanded that Buffalo Bills owner Ralph Wilson renegotiate his contract. He refused. The sportswriters and fans quickly chose a side—Wilson's. When O.J.'s name was announced fans lustily booed him. A bewildered O.J. "wondered where everything had gone." After his arrest he wouldn't have to wonder.[4]

II

The brutal murders of Nicole Brown Simpson and Ronald Goldman on June 12, 1994, did not initially change the public's benign view of O.J. Even as Los Angeles County district attorney Gil Garcetti prepared to charge him with the double murders, the O.J. mystique held. Two days after the murder, he was among the mourners at Nicole's funeral. There was no visible animosity toward him by her family. When O.J. made his by-now famous midday slow chase down the San Diego freeway after being charged with the murders, and dozens of LAPD cars followed him at a respectful distance, hundreds of white admirers cheered him and waved tattered, makeshift signs that read "Go Juice."

In polls by CNN immediately after his arrest, a majority of whites still believed that he was innocent. O.J. received more than seven thousand letters a day at the L.A. county jail offering him support and well-wishes.

The adulation didn't last long. O.J. may have been a media celebrity, sports icon, and all-American hero, but he was still a black man accused of murdering two whites, one a white female. Such accusations have always placed black men at risk. Throughout American history retribution against black men accused of murdering whites or raping white women has been swift and savage. In the O.J. case, race would continue to lurk dangerously close to the surface.

Garcetti quickly launched a relentless media trial of O.J. He tossed the presumption of innocence aside and treated O.J. as an escaped felon. He publicly proclaimed that "he had the right man" and that he expected him to confess. A quick succession of damaging leaks about O.J.'s relationship with Nicole, his "troubled" past, and his private life followed. The L.A. city attorney and the LAPD instantly turned over 911 tapes to the media in which O.J. screamed at and threatened Nicole.

The prosecution and press gleefully revealed that O.J. had pleaded guilty to assaulting Nicole in 1989. The prosecution skillfully painted O.J. as an irresponsible, abusive, and violent husband. The media hot on the scent of the big story took the cue and spun an even more sinister angle. *Time* called his relationship with Nicole "dangerous" and "dysfunctional." A companion article on Nicole in *Time* asked, "Is it her fault she's dead?" The implication was that her murder was the result of O.J.'s assaults on her.[5]

This propelled the issue of spousal abuse and domestic violence from bedroom privacy to public outrage. The hot lines at women's shelters jumped off the hook. The press deluged the public with angry editorials about domestic violence. Twenty-five states passed stiff laws mandating arrest and jail sentences for domestic assaults. Police, district attorneys, and judges nationwide promised to arrest, prosecute, and sentence domestic batterers.[6]

This was certainly welcome. But it was also hypocritical. For years, the press, the public, and politicians had turned a deaf ear to the issue of domestic violence. They took lightning action now because America's most famous batterer was a black man. Even though the majority of child molesters, serial killers, domestic assailants, and rapists are white or nonblack males, O.J. joined Deh Judge (Clarence Thomas), Mel (dirty phone sex) Reynolds, and the two Mikes (Jackson and Tyson) on the list of prominent black men who had become America's poster boys for sexual deviancy. This fed the timeworn myth that black men are exclusively America's sexual miscreants.

III

The mainstream media loved it. They took the sleaze tabloids' favorite obsessions—sex, drugs, violence, the antics of high-profile celebrities—and eagerly applied their smut techniques to O.J. It was soon hard to distinguish their reports on O.J. from those in the *Star, Examiner,* and *National Enquirer.*

Note: And why not? The O.J. case generated an estimated domestic gross product of $200 million. This was far more than the GDP of many African nations. The only thing missing from "O.J. Inc." was a CEO, CFO, board chair, and stockholders. The media sopped up a lot of that gravy. In 1994, the National Enquirer *smeared O.J. gossip and lies across twenty-one of twenty-seven cover stories. Sales zoomed to an estimated 500,000 weekly. When the tabs didn't put Juice trash on the cover, sales plunged 30 percent.* Newsweek, Time, People, U.S. News & World Report, Sports Illustrated, Atlantic Monthly *and* *the* New Yorker *heard the cash registers hum and tossed in a generous supply of O.J. on their covers or inside pages.*[7]

Time admitted that it doctored O.J.'s cover photo to make him look more sinister. When blacks protested, *Time*'s managing editor at first blamed the distorted photo on a freelance artist commissioned by the magazine.

This explanation satisfied no one. Black journalists confronted the editor at a conference cosponsored by the National Association of Black Journalists. They called the distorted cover "a racist act." The editor backed away—slightly. He denied that any "racial implication was intended." He insisted that it was an editorial decision that newspapers and magazines make all the time. They routinely crop, touch up, and retouch the pictures of politicians, personalities, and even Presidents for satirical or caricature affect.[8]

The *Time* cover was not satire. There were no space considerations to consider. There was no artistic reason to create a different mood. *Time* did not tamper with two pictures of convicted mass murderer Jeffrey Dahmer. He is shown as a sad-eyed, contrite young man. (Nor did *Time* touch up its cover photo of Ollie North or executed serial killer John Wayne Gacy.)

Newsweek magazine made public the issue that many had whispered in private about: black men and white women. In a cover story entitled "The Double Life of O. J. Simpson," *Newsweek* ran a cropped photo that showed two persons, a bikini-clad young white woman in a sexually suggestive pose and O. J. Simpson leering at her. The caption read "duty and obsession." O.J.'s alleged obsession was his pathological "lust after only white women."[9]

America's oldest and most deadly taboo, interracial sex, was now out in the open. Many whites pretended that race didn't matter in love and marriage. It did. A 1991 poll by the National Research Center of 1,500 Americans found that 66 percent of whites opposed a close relative marrying a black man.[10]

Many blacks, especially women, although they publicly supported him and believed he was innocent/framed/part of a conspiracy to get a black man, were livid that he married Nicole. He provided her with an elegant lifestyle. They lived in a multi million-dollar mansion and maintained a private apartment and condo. They spent thousands of dollars on clothes, jewelry, jet-set vacations, and gambling junkets to Las Vegas. Many blacks viewed O.J. as another sad example of a prominent black man who had turned his back on his community, his people, and his women.

Note: The question is often asked: "What if the murder victim had been Marguerite and not Nicole?" Marguerite was O.J.'s first wife. She is black. Would millions have been mesmerized by the case for months on end? Would the press have tumbled over itself to get every snatch of O.J. gossip? Would the networks have fought pitched battles to get TV cameras into the courtroom? Would the prosecution have spent an estimated $7–9 million to nail him? And finally, the most cynical question of all: would he have even been arrested? I did not hear one black or a considerable number of whites who raised that question ever answer yes to all of the above.

IV

Meanwhile, the prosecution and the media made public more charges of domestic violence by him. There were reports that the DNA tests on drops of blood found at the murder scene and in O.J.'s car matched Nicole's and Goldman's. Nicole's sisters made teary-eyed, well-publicized appearances on TV talk shows accusing him of murder.

This hardened the racial lines. The majority of whites believed he was guilty. The issue for them was murder, not race. The majority of blacks still believed that he was innocent or was framed "by unknown forces." They insisted that the case against him was part of an ongoing racist conspiracy to "get" blacks.

O.J. and the defense team publicly pledged that race "would not be a part of the trial." Yet they did much to make sure that it was. O.J.'s pricey, "dream team" attorneys pushed hard to discredit LAPD lieutenant Mark Fuhrman. He was one of the first officers at the crime scene. He claimed to have found the bloody glove during a search of the grounds outside O.J.'s home. Defense attorneys repeatedly pointed to Fuhrman's alleged history of racist remarks and violent actions toward blacks. They implied that he planted the glove to frame O.J.

At a pretrial hearing in mid-January, the issue of race exploded. Black deputy assistant district attorney Christopher Darden defended Fuhrman against charges of racism. This touched off a prolonged and heated exchange with Simpson codefense counsel Johnnie Cochran over the use of the "N" word, racial epithets, and sexual relations between black men and white women.

Note: Darden was only doing his job in trying to convict O.J. But Darden had no illusions that he was exempt from the racist stereotypes about black men. Witness this exchange with an interviewer:

> *Q. Do black prosecutors face any special burdens either inside or outside the courtroom?*
>
> *D. On more than one occasion I've walked into court and the judge has mistaken me for the public defender.*
>
> *Q. Has the judge ever mistaken you for a defendant?*
>
> *D. Yes, as a matter of fact, now that you mention it.*

Darden was applauded by the press, patted on the back by much of the public, lauded by the legal profession; and his book, In Contempt, became an instant best seller. But the stark and bitter reality was that to the men who call the shots in the criminal justice system only the thinnest of lines separated Darden from the black fallen idol he was prosecuting, as well as from other black men he had prosecuted.[11]

After months of endless media gossip, speculation, rumors, and defense and prosecution leaks, the question was, Could O.J. get a fair trial? If O.J.'s pockets were deep enough he might. Cochran was blunt: "The costs are going to be major." He estimated that the Simpson defense would cost a minimum of two million dollars. O.J. relinquished his board membership in four corporations and liquidated more than two million dollars in stock and options he held in the companies to defray legal costs. O.J. showed that there was still a lot of juice left in "the Juice" when it came to raising quick cash to pay his legal expenses. He raked in about one to three million dollars (depending on whom you want to believe) through the sale of his book *I Want To Tell You,* which presented his version of the events.[12]

O.J.'s best hope for acquittal rested on getting as many blacks as possible on the jury. His defense attorneys hired a top jury consulting firm, Trial Logistics, to devise a questionnaire to weed out racially biased jurors. O.J. had an advantage. He was tried in the Central District Court of Los Angeles County which had the highest percentage of jury-eligible blacks in the County.[13]

Note: The trial ripped the racial blinders off O.J.'s eyes. In fact, he did a volte-face from his life of racial denial and saw race everywhere. He obsessively counted the number of blacks, Hispanics, and Asians in the courtroom and screamed to everyone within earshot that "racism is part of the trial." If it had gone on much longer, O.J. might have shown up in court wearing a black suit and a bow tie.[14]

V

Following weeks of skirmishing between prosecutors and defense attorneys, marred by charges of racism, juror intimidation, and manipulation, nine of the final twelve jurors selected were black. Despite the silly and in more than a few cases bigoted rantings of many media and legal talking-head experts that blacks would never convict another black, there was never any hard guarantee the jurors would acquit him—blacks are just as worried about crime and tough on criminals as whites. O.J. understood this. He didn't believe that black jurors would hustle in a slam-dunk verdict for acquittal. "You see black jurors putting black people in jail daily."[15]

The defense trial strategy was simple: charge that the LAPD did not search for other suspects and the district attorney rushed to judgment in prosecuting Simpson, challenge the reliability of the DNA tests, strongly hint that there was a police conspiracy to frame him, depict Simpson and Nicole as a couple with normal marital difficulties, accuse the DA of tainting evidence, and subtly play the race card to sway the black jurors toward Simpson.

The jurors bought it. But not for the reason that many talking-head media commentators and legal analysts not so sneakily implied—racism-in-reverse. The jurors repeatedly told anyone who would listen that they made their decision strictly on the basis of facts, testimony, and physical evidence (or lack thereof). There was not a shred of proof that they "nullified" the evidence and let a "brother" walk solely because he was a "brother." [16]

It didn't matter what the black jurors said; much of America believed they did. (There were two white jurors and one Latino juror. They were conveniently forgotten.) Clinton tipped the angry mood when he asked Americans to "show sympathy for the victims." As for the verdict, he asked only that Americans "respect" it. He never said accept it. O.J. was acquitted in a court of law but he would forever stand convicted in the court of public opinion. [17]

In much of America's view, O.J. was a black man who committed a heinous crime and used fame and wealth to buy a dream-team defense to mangle the system and evade his just due. The boycott and backlash against him as individual and symbol were on with a vengeance. He was a corporate untouchable, a media pariah, and the object of public wrath.

O.J. didn't quite get the message. He apparently thought that the media was exaggerating the hostility against him. He thought that a few happy face promotional appearances and a heavily hyped TV interview would restore the old O.J.-running-through-airports image. It took massive demonstrations by women's groups, a canceled pay-per-view program, and thousands of angry calls that forced O.J. and NBC to cancel the scheduled interview to slap him out of his near-comatose hallucination that he could win back public acceptance.

O.J. licked his wounds and withdrew from public view for a

while. When he finally resurfaced, he had concluded that the only place he would have a semblance of a chance to tell his story was on Black Entertainment TV. "Brother" Simpson was finally forced to "come back home." [18]

Note: I didn't forget about the "O.J. Tells All Video." For $29.95 plus shipping and handling you could see and hear O.J. pour out his soul and swear that he didn't do anything. The problem was that to much of the public it smacked of a desperate put-up job to make a quick buck. The public wasn't moved and the media wasn't about to relent. Not one major network or local station would take a penny of, as one called it, O.J. "blood money" to advertise the tape.[19]

In other well-timed media appearances O.J. smiled and was gracious and humble, but it didn't change anyone's mind. Those who thought he was guilty still thought he was guilty. The media didn't relent. It kept the media spotlight on the suffering of the Brown family and the emotional appeal by the Goldmans for justice. This sent even more whites rushing to the moral barricades. As O.J. continued to discover, the case punched too many emotional hot buttons and pricked too many social sores. The wrongful-death suits would dog him through the courts for months after his acquittal.

There are lessons to be learned from the Simpson saga. O.J. was a beloved sports icon. He played the corporate game. He lived a princely lifestyle. He had what appeared to be a charmed marriage. But in the end he was a man who symbolized everything but stood for nothing. He was a black man who discovered the hard way that wealth, fame, and status can't buy any black a passport or exemption from racial and sexual stereotyping.

O.J. will fight to the bitter end to do what he can to rehabilitate his image and turn white contempt into, at best, white indifference. He may succeed a little. But there will always be those who will stop, turn their heads, point their finger, and whisper "Murderer" when he walks by. It's not fair but that's the terrible price he must pay for his freedom.

Chapter 17

Countering the Assassination of the Black Male Image

I was jogging along the street near my home early one morning. When I stopped at an intersection to wait for the traffic light to change I caught the eye of a driver, a young white woman. She looked nervous and frightened. In a quick move she snapped down the lock on her car door and sped off before the light changed.

This was not the first time that I was the object of suspicion by fearful whites. I have been followed by security guards and clerks in stores. Women have clutched their purses when I approached. Cab drivers have refused to pick me up. I've been stopped and questioned by the police even though I wore a suit and tie and drove a late-model car. There's nothing unusual about this. Many black males tell the same story. They have become a routine part of American folklore. It's one more symptom of America's deep fear of black males.

But there's more. A few months after the jogging incident, I sat in the parking lot of an office building waiting for a business acquaintance to arrive. A young black man approached my car. He was neatly dressed. You guessed it. My first impulse was to lock my car door and roll up the window. It turned out that he was only trying to locate another office building on the same street.

As he walked away I thought of the woman who locked her door when she saw me. Her fear of black men had also become my fear. The image of black criminality, violence, and depravity has been rammed so deep into America's collective psyche that no one is immune from fear. That includes many blacks like myself. Can anything be done to counter the terrifying image of the black male? Yes!

II
THE MEDIA

It is the most powerful medium in the world. It shapes public attitudes and opinions. When it recycles the standard crime/drug/violence/gang/dereliction story on the "hood," don't just read it, shake your head, complain to the walls, or worse, accept it as the sacred word.

• Write a letter, send a fax or an e-mail, or make a phone call to the reporter or editor. Describe a black rite of passage, mentoring program, academic achievement or scholarship award ceremony, or a student honors program. Nine out of ten (probably more) young blacks aren't into gangs, drugs, or crime. They are part of these events.

• Invite reporters to come out and cover these events. Tell them that this is news, too. When they tell you it isn't and that it won't sell, remind them that any story can be made newsworthy. Send them clippings of young white kids riding skateboards; romping on the beach; playing in chess tournaments; participating in academic decathlons; winning awards in music, drama, and science competitions; and creating innovative science projects. Let them know that there are many young blacks that are doing the same.

• Praise reporters or editors when they write the rare feature or news story that spotlights black achievement and excellence. Let them know that there's much more where that came from.

• The media is a cash cow. Sponsors and advertisers influence the content of news and programming. Conservative and Christian fundamentalist groups understand this. They bombard them with letters, faxes, e-mail, and phone calls. They threaten to protest, picket, and boycott them. Their goal is to get programs on that reflect their politics, point-of-view, and agenda and to get programs off that don't. They have been monstrously successful. When in living memory has there been a documentary or special that advocates, fully explains, or simply presents a favorable opinion or two on the issue of abortion or the right to choice on the air?

If it works for these groups it can work for those who want to eliminate stereotypical programming. There are a few positive examples. When the Fox network announced that it would cancel the popular series *Roc,* blacks sent thousands of angry letters demanding that Fox keep *Roc* on the air. They didn't but it made Fox pause and think for a moment about its decision. But one spontaneous letter-writing campaign is not enough. There has to a consistent ongoing focused campaign to pressure the network managers and newspaper editors to air more positive programs and print more stories on black achievement. That takes organization, time, patience, and dedication.

• Blacks potentially have the economic power and clout to apply pressure and influence advertisers. They are the ultimate consumers in America. They spend an estimated $300 billion annually on goods and services. Corporations get the lion's share of black dollars. When corporate sponsors and advertisers are reminded of that they must listen.

Several black groups proved this when they threatened a boycott campaign against the record companies that market "gangsta" rap. Atlantic Records gave in and agreed to cease distributing these records. Although other companies quickly took up the distribution slack, the groups' success showed that when a company perceives a threat to its bottom line it will listen and even act.

• The civil rights movement was enormously successful with another tactic: protest. It can work with the media. The few times that blacks have thrown up picket lines around a newspaper (protesting biased news coverage), a movie theater (demeaning film), radio station (hate talk jocks), and TV station (lack of black managers, anchors, or technical staff), they have forced management to make changes or at least consider them. They can challenge the licenses of radio and TV stations. While license challenges are nearly impossible to win they can force the FCC to investigate the complaints or even to hold a hearing. This gives advocacy groups a public platform to air grievances and complaints.

The NAACP has occasionally held hearings on discrimination in personnel hiring practices and racially biased program content in the media. It has been effective in drawing press attention to bias in the studios and newsrooms, but rarely has it had a lasting impact.

• At times blacks have formed local ad hoc media watchdog groups to protest a racially offensive program or programmer. These have been almost always single-issue actions. They disappear quickly. A national black media watchdog organization should be formed to monitor editorial and program content, consult with sponsors and advertisers, and advise publishers, editors, reporters, and radio and TV station managers about minority hiring and promotions. It can suggest features and news ideas and maintain a data bank of competent and dedicated black professionals as potential hires or consultants to help develop news stories, features, commentaries, and PSA spots.

• Cable public-access TV has the potential to reach millions. The FCC hasn't yet put crushing limits on who and what can be aired. Here is a fertile area to create positive programs that educate and inform the local community.

• The Internet is the communications tool of the future. Internet users can establish worldwide links with millions. They can participate in chat sessions, suggest pertinent readings, journals, newsletters, and articles, form study groups, promote and market products, and keep others informed about local news and activities. Suggestion: get hooked up!

• Railing at the "white media" for perpetuating negative images of blacks misses the point. Much of the black press is often guilty of the same. There is one black-owned TV station, roughly 150-plus black-owned radio stations, and 250-plus black-published newspapers nationally. If they titillate black readers with crime and violence stories, exclusively tout athletes and entertainers as role models, and ignore black scholarship and achievement, they are just as harmful as the "white media" they criticize. They can offer interviews and news features on black scholars, scientists, academics, artists, historical figures, civic and religious leaders, and community activists. We need to know their ideas, programs, and accomplishments. They are the authentic role models and heroes in their communities.

III
JUST SAY NO

Nancy Reagan isn't the only one who can use this slogan. The best way to say no to harmful stereotypes and destructive media images and those who propagate them is not to spend a penny on them. Here are my don'ts.

- Don't buy records, tapes, and videos that call black women "bitches" and "hos," black men "gangstas," and blacks "niggas." (Far more rappers don't say these things than do.)
- Don't buy tickets to plays and comedy acts that demean, trash, and pander to the profane under the guise of humor or theater.
- Don't spend every waking hour watching mindless sit-coms that resemble Amos and Andy, Sapphire, and Kingfish rituals.
- Don't encourage friends, relatives, and acquaintances (including yourself) to participate in spectacles of degradation sometimes known as daytime TV talk shows. You may get fifteen seconds of fame but black people get a lifetime of shame.
- Don't buy books that substitute cheap sex thrills for honest attempts to assess and grapple with love and relationships between men and women; that trash *all,*

most, or *the majority* of black men; or glorify the "gangsta" lifestyle as the black lifestyle.

- Don't bankroll Hollywood's vision of the hood. Remember, blacks buy an estimated one out of four movie tickets. Hollywood, if given its way, will never have a shortage of roles that depict blacks as updated versions of Toms, clowns, coons, crooks, mulattos, mammies, and bucks.

The list of dos is simple:

- Support every author, artist, performer, and product that reverses all of the above.

IV
DO FOR SELF

There was a time when the only places where one could find the small number of black-oriented books, records, videos, and tapes were the major chain book, record, and video stores. Not anymore.

- There are thousands of black bookstores, video shops, and record shops nationally. They can become a positive and innovative outlet for positive black-oriented products.

- Authors, recording artists, entertainers, and media personalities should regularly schedule promotional appearances at black-owned book, video, and record stores. A good example is General Powell. He made it a special point to schedule an appearance at a black-owned book store in San Bernardino, California, during his national tour. It was a huge success. It drew hundreds of customers to a store that they would never have had a clue existed.

- Employ nontraditional product marketing techniques. Grocery, department and hardware stores, beauty and barber shops, gas stations, and car washes now sell books, records, tapes, and videos. They can carry positive black-oriented books, records, tapes, and videos, too.

• In the chapter "Why Are They Waiting to Exhale?," I mentioned that mainstream publishers showed *zero* interest in publishing my book on positive black male parenting, *Black Fatherhood: The Guide to Male Parenting.* I didn't beg, plead, weep, wail, blame, and cuss out "the white man" for not publishing it. A small black-owned publishing company, Middle Passage Press, did. The publisher was hardworking and persistent. It bucked the massive barrier erected by the New York publishing biggies and the mainstream media that ignores small-press books. It successfully marketed the book. It pried open the doors at the chain bookstores, got a national distributor, and eventually got some sympathetic publicity from columnists (not reviewers; most of them still take their marching orders from the New York publishing crowd). It helped me. It helped a black business grow. It provided an encouraging model for success for other blacks.

V
DON'T ASSASSINATE YOUR OWN IMAGE

I often hear my black friends, acquaintances, and relatives (yes, I include myself) make blanket indictments of young blacks. They say they lack morals, manners, and motivation, and are violent and crime-prone. In short we routinely and ignorantly repeat one or more of the stereotypes about ourselves. Blacks will say these negative things while their own sons and daughters sit in the same room doing their homework, studying, and reading. Their children represent the overwhelming majority of blacks who don't do drugs, join gangs, commit crime, or make babies and problems. What message does that send to your own children? Worse, what message does that send to the adults who hurl the insults at them?

I can understand why many blacks believe the stereotypes about themselves, even though they know that most blacks don't fit any of them. Blacks watch the same TV programs, read the same newspapers, listen to the same radio programs that practically from the cradle to grave throb with and reinforce racial and gender stereotypes. It is virtually impossible to be immune from this social pollution.

- The first step in the racial stereotype self-cleansing process is to be aware of what you say and do.
- The second step is to become a talking, walking, thinking, and most importantly acting antistereotype and role model around family, friends, in organizations, in your place of business, and at school.
- The third step is to get involved in church, civic, political, PTA, fraternities, sororities, associations, rites-of-passage and mentoring programs, and anywhere else where you can set a positive example of excellence and achievement.

These are only suggestions. But if we take one or more of them they will go a long way toward countering the self-hateful, self-destructive, and ultimately self-defeating images many Americans have of blacks and many blacks have of themselves.

America's Hidden Agenda Against Black Males: A Postscript

I sometimes forget about how many Americans see black men. That's why I got excited when Carol called to tell me that she had convinced her story editor at National Public Radio to do a Father's Day feature in 1993 on "three generations of black men." Carol, who works as a freelance producer for NPR, wanted to interview me, my father, and my son.

Carol assured me that this would not be another crime-drug-gangs-poverty-dereliction story about black men. To get a good family feel, she suggested that she tape us during a family dinner. She would get some ambient sound while we ate and conversed. After dinner, she would do the taping.

Carol was very thorough. She spent several hours discussing our family's concerns and achievements. She wanted listeners to feel the warmth and love that we felt for each other.

A few days later, Carol called and thanked me. She said that the material was great. A day later, she called again. She told me that her editor decided not to air the program on Father's Day. NPR wanted something a "little lighter." She again assured me that they liked the material. The red flag inched up higher in my mind.

Over the next few weeks, Carol called several times. She assured me that NPR was still interested but that she was now working with another editor who wanted more background material. Each time I asked her if she had a tentative air date. Carol said that NPR rarely gave producers specific air dates for features. Two months and three editors later, Carol assured me that NPR was still interested, but she had another new editor who wanted to refocus the feature. What the hell did that mean? She was vague. I told her that they were jerking her around. She weakly protested that they still wanted to do something.

They probably did. They simply didn't have a clue how to handle a story spotlighting the successes of black men. NPR, along with much of the media, had built an impregnable tomb and locked itself in. If the story is not crime, drugs, gangs, or poverty they're lost. Carol reluctantly agreed. The story never aired.

Note: It took some doing but NPR finally did discover that there was more to the "hood" than guns, gangs, drugs, poverty, degradation, and dysfunctionality. It did several features and reports on black men achieving and contributing to their communities. I'm happy to say that I participated in some of the programs.

II

Shortly after the NPR fiasco, the Anti-Defamation League revealed that 31 percent of young whites between eighteen and thirty years old thought blacks were lazy and violence-prone. The political pundits seemed surprised. I was, too. I was surprised the percentage was that low. When young whites read the papers and watch TV news programs, do they see regular features on successful, prosperous black business, professional, and craft persons, artists, and political leaders? Or do they see black males bent over police cars, or sitting in court, prison, and juvenile halls? Do they see almost daily photo shots of young black scholars? Or do they see muglike shots of young black males as dope dealers, drive-by shooters, gang-bangers, and car-jackers?

My guess is that many more young whites secretly believe that blacks are lazy and violence prone. They are just too diplomatic to say it. Some people still consider it impolite to admit that they think and believe the worst about blacks.[1]

It's a pity, too, because thirty years ago blacks defied water hoses, police dogs, and police billy clubs. They sang, prayed, and marched against Jim Crow laws. It was good versus evil. Whites applauded them and called them the "moral conscience" of America. Those days are long gone. The applause has been replaced by fear of and hysteria toward black men. It's affected everyone. And there's a reason.

The Reagan-Bush administration's slash and burn of social programs and Gingrich, Pat Buchanan, and company's scorched-earth ultraconservative political assault was not just mean-spirited. It tapped the huge reservoir of racial know-nothingness that has always slinked beneath the surface in American society while legitimizing and elevating racial scapegoating to national policy. In an era of scarcity and declining resources, the search for enemies is ruthless. Blacks are the oldest and most visible enemy. They are the softest of soft targets.[2]

If Americans think that black males are inherently stupid, there's no need to build more schools, hire more teachers, provide advanced materials, state-of-the-art equipment, and a college prep curriculum for them. If Americans think that black males are gang members, drive-by shooters, and dope dealers, there's no need to spend more on job and skills training and entrepreneurial programs for them. If Americans think that black men are absentee or irresponsible fathers, there's no need to overhaul and strengthen welfare and income-maintenance programs to ensure greater family support systems for them.

If Americans think that black males are chronic alcoholics, druggies, and disease risks, there's no need to support a national health care program for the poor and uninsured. If Americans believe that black males are derelict and immoral, Presidents and political leaders won't say "We shall overcome" and won't propose stronger civil rights laws, increased affirmative action programs, and greater civil liberties protections.[3]

If Americans believe that young black males are a menace to society, they will pay for armies of police, prosecutors, chain gangs, fortress-like prisons, and repressive laws, and shrilly call for sending the National Guard into the ghettos while gutting social programs and bankrupting cities. Many police and public officials in saner moments privately admit that none of this has made a dent in crime or the streets any safer.[4]

But, they can't stop. So blacks are caught in a Catch-22. When they complain, they are told to stop yapping about racism and poverty and start cleaning up their own communities. When sympathetic whites complain, they are told that liberalism is dead or that when they get mugged they'll be talking about "those people," too. When sympathetic Jews complain, they are told that blacks are anti-Semitic. When sympathetic Latinos and Asians complain, they are told to watch out, blacks will take your jobs and burn down your stores. It's victim-blaming with a vengeance.

The saddest part of this is that many blacks have swallowed the poison of racism. Many black men don't call black women "sister." They call them "bitches" and "hos." Many black men don't call other black men "brothers." They call them "nigger" and "bitch." Many black women don't call black men "brother" either. They call them "dogs," "animals," and "bastards." Many black women don't call black men "sweetheart" and "lover." They call them "brutes and batterers." Many black men don't respect and revere their parents and elders. They demean or terrorize them.

The moment many black men and women have an extra dollar, they head for the farthest suburbs, cross their fingers, and pray that no one burns a cross on their lawn or calls their children "nigger" in the schools. Many black leaders will spend as much time calling for more police, prisons, and boot camps as they do calling for jobs, education, and health programs. Meanwhile, those left behind in the ghettos get poorer, angrier, and more desperate.

The black unity that many blacks talked and dreamed about during the 1960s has become a fractured nightmare. I can't say that evil men plotted or scripted all this in a backroom. Things never work that way. They don't have to. The assassination of the black male image has transformed black men into the universal bogeyman. The trick is to transform them back into universal human beings. If not, writer Charles Carroll, who confidently told the world a century ago that the black man was a beast, may yet have the last word.

Notes

The Growth Industry in Black Male Mythology: An Overview

1. *Los Angeles Times,* October 17, 1995, p. 12.
2. *Los Angeles Times,* May 21, 1995, p. 1; Sept. 21, 1995, p. 22.
3. Margo Walker, "Black Students Just Say No," *Emerge,* August 1991, p. 4.
4. Michelle Ingrassia, "A World Without Fathers," *Newsweek,* August 23, 1993, pp. 17–27.
5. "Whites' Myths About Blacks," *U.S. News & World Report,* November 9, 1992, pp. 41–44; Janine Jackson, "Talk Radio: Who Gets to Talk," *Extra!,* April/May 1993, pp. 14–17; Thomas F. Pettigrew, "New Politics of Racism," *Rutgers Law Review* 37 Summer 1985, 685–91.
6. Andrew Billingsley, *Climbing Jacob's Ladder: The Enduring Legacy of African-American Families* (New York: Simon & Schuster, 1992), pp. 147–69.
7. Sheryl Stolberg and Stephanie Gross, "Gunfire Deaths of

Black Teens in Stark Rise," *Los Angeles Times,* June 10, 1992, p. 1; Greg Krikorian, "Study Questions Justice System's Racial Fairness," *Los Angeles Times,* February 13, 1996, p. 1.

1. The Negro: A Beast . . . or in the Image of God?

1. Eric Lichtblau, "King Discusses Beating with Students," *Los Angeles Times,* November 19, 1992, p. 3.
2. *Los Angeles Times,* April 30, 1992, p. 1; May 1, 1992, p. 5.
3. *Los Angeles Times,* November 20, 1992, p. 1.
4. James Rainey, "A Man of Conflicting Images," *Los Angeles Times,* August 3, 1995, p. 1.
5. Richard Bardolph, ed., *The Civil Rights Record, Black America and the Law, 1849–1870* (New York: Thomas Y. Crowell, Co., 1970), p. 102.
6. Ibid., pp. 103–104.
7. Harvey Wish, ed., *Ante-Bellum* (New York: Capricorn Books, 1960), pp. 14, 89.
8. Kenneth O'Reilly, *Nixon's Piano: Presidents and Racial Politics from Washington to Clinton* (New York: Free Press, 1995), pp. 16, 21, 28, 30.
9. Forrest G. Wood, *The Black Scare: The Racist Response to Emancipation and Reconstruction* (Berkeley: University of California Press, 1968), pp. 1–79.
10. Eric Foner, *Reconstruction* (New York: Harper & Row, 1988).
11. George M. Frederickson, *The Black Image in the White Mind, 1817–1914* (New York: Harper & Row, 1971), pp. 249, 281, 251.
12. Ibid., p. 253.
13. Rayford Logan, "The Negro as Portrayed in Representative Northern Magazines and Newspapers," in Barry N. Schwartz and Robert Disch, eds., *White Racism* (New York: Dell Publishing, 1970), p. 395.
14. Bardolph, p. 107.

15. C. Vann Woodward, *The Strange Career of Jim Crow* (New York: Oxford University Press, 1957), p. 78.

16. Charles Murray, *The Bell Curve* (New York: Free Press, 1994), pp. 340, 522; Dinesh D'Souza, *The End of Racism* (New York: Free Press, 1995), pp. 91, 179, 477.

17. Upton Sinclair, *The Jungle* (1906. Reprint. New York: New American Library, 1964), p. 270.

18. Frederickson, pp. 260, 280–81.

19. Seymour L. Gross and John Edward Hardy, *The Image of the Negro in American Literature* (Chicago: University of Chicago Press, 1966), p. 80.

20. O'Reilly, p. 90.

21. Donald Boggle, *Toms, Coons, Mulattos, Mammies and Bucks* (New York: Continuum Publishing Co., 1989), pp. 8, 10.

22. Robert L. Zangrando, *The NAACP Crusade Against Lynching, 1909–1950* (Philadelphia: Temple University, 1980), pp. 6–7.

23. *Thirty Years of Lynching, 1889–1918* (New York: NAACP, 1919), p. 36.

24. *The Works of Theodore Roosevelt,* Vol. 17 (New York: Charles Scribner & Sons, 1925), pp. 411–15.

25. Logan, p. 397.

26. W. E. B. Du Bois, "Mob Tactics," *Crisis* 34, August 1927, 204.

27. Frederickson, p. 274.

28. Michael L. Radelet, "Executions of Whites for Crimes Against Blacks: Exceptions to the Rule?," *Sociological Quarterly,* 30, 1989, 529–44.

29. Logan, pp. 393, 396.

30. Alfred McClung Lee and Royal D. Colle, "The Negro Image and the Mass Media," Ph.D dissertation, Cornell University, 1967.

31. Robert H. Ferrell, ed., *Letters to Bess* (New York: W. W. Norton, 1983), pp. 341, 385, 421–22.

32. Earl Warren, *The Memoirs of Earl Warren* (New York: Doubleday, 1977), pp. 291–92.

33. O'Reilly, pp. 292, 277–329.

34. Ibid., p. 377; "Falling Behind: A Report on How Blacks Have Fared Under Reagan," *Journal of Black Studies* 17, December 1986, 148–72; Martin A. Lee and Norman Soloman, *Unreliable Sources: A Guide to Detecting Bias in News Media* (New York: Carol Publishing Group, 1990), pp. 238–44.
35. *Los Angeles Times,* December 9, 1995, p. 6; *USA Today,* February 16, 1996, p. 3.

2. The Fine Art of Black Male Bashing

1. Joe Sharkey, *Deadly Greed: The Stuart Murder Case in Boston and the 1980's in America* (New York: Prentice-Hall, 1991), pp. 124, 126, 137, 136, 144; Larry Martz, "A Murderous Hoax," *Newsweek,* January 22, 1990, pp. 16–22.
2. *New York Times,* October 28, 1995, p. 7.
3. Martz, p. 22.
4. David Anderson, *Crime and the Politics of Hysteria: How the Willie Horton Story Changed American Justice* (book review), *Progressive,* October 1995, p. 41.
5. David Shaw, "What's the News? White Editors Make the Call," *Los Angeles Times,* December 13, 1990, p. 1.
6. David Halberstam, *The Powers That Be* (New York: Alfred A. Knopf, 1979), pp. 62, 267, 205, 216.
7. Barbara Reynolds, "The Media Flunks," *USA Today,* March 1, 1996, p. 10; Shaw, op. cit.
8. Ben Bagdikian, *The Media Monopoly* (Boston: Beacon Press, 1990); David Shaw, "Negative News and Little Else," *Los Angeles Times,* December 11, 1990, p. 1.
9. *New York Times,* August 25, 1993, p. B1; Ronald Brownstein, "Clinton, Bush Step Up Debate on Family Values," *Los Angeles Times,* May 22, 1992, p. 22; Douglas Jehl, "Quayle Deplores Eroding Values," *Los Angeles Times,* May 20, 1992, p. 1; Dave Marsh, "Cops N' Gangstas," *Nation,* June 26, 1995, p. 908.

10. *Los Angeles Times,* February 2, 1996, p. F19.

11. Rochelle Sharp, "In Latest Recession Only Blacks Suffered Net Income Loss," *Wall Street Journal,* September 14, 1993, p. 1; Billy J. Tidwell, "A Profile of the Black Unemployed," in *State of Black America, 1987* (New York: Urban League, 1987), p. 236; "Urban Poverty Expert Talks About Causes," *Los Angeles Wave,* September 18, 1993, p. 1.

12. Jeannye Thornton and David Whitman, "Whites' Myths About Blacks," *U.S. News & World Report,* November 9, 1992, pp. 41–44.

13. *Time,* November 14, 1994, pp. 43–48.

14. Sharkey, p. 235.

3. From Slavery to the Sports Arena

1. *New York Times,* January 16, 1988, p. 47; *New York Times,* January 26, 1988, Sec. II, p. 8.

2. Frederick Douglass, *Life and Times of Frederick Douglass,* (1842; New York: Collier Books, 1962), p. 148.

3. Arthur Ashe, Jr., *A Hard Road to Glory: A History of the Black Athlete, 1619–1918,* vol. 1 (New York: World Books, 1988), pp. 19–21.

4. Tony Gilmore, *Bad Nigger! The National Impact of Jack Johnson* (Port Washington, N.Y.: Kennikat Press, 1975).

5. Harry Edwards, *The Revolt of the Black Athlete* (New York: The Free Press, 1970); William Oscar Johnson, "The Black Athlete Revisited," *Sports Illustrated,* August 5, 1991, p. 40.

6. Leroy D. Clark, "Is It Time to Change the Playing Field?" *Emerge,* October 1994, pp. 56, 59.

7. *Los Angeles Times,* January 3, 1996, p. C4.

8. *Los Angeles Times,* February 2, 1996, p. C3; February 13, 1996, p. C5; Denise Gellene, "Will Magic Make a Comeback to Product Pitchman?," *Los Angeles Times,* February 2, 1996, p. D1.

9. *Los Angeles Times,* September 17, 1983, Sec. VI, p. 1.
10. Jackie Robinson, *I Never Had It Made* (New York: G. P. Putnam, 1972).

4. Doing the Wrong Thing by Spike

1. Earl Ofari Hutchinson, "Racial Double Standard Puts Spike Lee at a Disadvantage," *Los Angeles Times,* June 8, 1992, p. 3.
2. Earl Ofari Hutchinson, "Are Blacks Still Colored in Hollywood?," *Los Angeles Sentinel,* February 21, 1996, p. 6.
3. See Daniel J. Leab, *From Sambo to Superspade: The Black Experience in Motion Pictures* (Boston: Houghton-Mifflin, 1975).
4. *Spike Lee's Gotta Have It* (New York: Simon and Schuster, 1987), pp. 316–17.
5. *Habla Malcolm X* (New York: Pathfinder Press, 1993), p. 108.

5. Thomas, Tyson, and Tall Tales

1. *Los Angeles Times,* November 10, 1993, p. 1; Ellen Bravo, "Sexual Harassment," *Service Employees Union* 6, Winter 1992, pp. 16–17.
2. E. J. Dionne, Jr., "Schism in the Black Community Brought to Bar," *New York Times,* July 4, 1991, p. 1; *Washington Post,* August 9, 1991, p. 1.
3. Kim Deterline, "Double Standards in Domestic Violence Coverage," *Extra!,* July-August 1994, p. 6.
4. See Donald Boggle, *Toms, Coons, Mulattos, Mammies and Bucks* (New York: Continuum Publishing Co., 1989).
5. Helene Cooper, "A Question of Justice: Do Prosecutors Target Minority Politicians?" *Wall Street Journal,* January 12, 1996, p. 1.
6. Charles Murray, "The Coming White Underclass," *Wall Street Journal,* October 29, 1993, p. 12; Elizabeth Mehren,

"So Who Are those Unwed Mothers?" *Los Angeles Times,* October 30, 1995, p. E1, "The New Single Motherhood," *Los Angeles Times,* November 9, 1995, p. E5.

7. Earl Ofari Hutchinson, "Tyson Brought Up Images Black Men Can't Ignore," *Guardian,* March 11, 1992, p. 18; Jose Torres, *Fear and Fire* (New York: New American Library, 1989).

8. Kweku Hanson, "Racial Disparities and the Law of Death: The Case for a New Hard Look at Race-Based Challenges to Capital Punishment," *National Black Law Journal* 2, 1990, 299–302; Hugo A. Bedeau, *Capital Punishment in the United States* (New York: Oxford University Press, 1982), pp. 107–19.

9. *New York Times,* August 13, 1991, p. 31.

10. Bill Turque, "Judgment for the Wilders," *Newsweek,* August 27, 1990, p. 30.

11. *Los Angeles Times,* January 11, 1996, p. 3; February 8, 1996, p. B4; February 4, 1996, p. B4.

12. *Los Angeles Times,* October 13, 1991, p. 31.

13. *Othello,* Act I, Scene I; Winthrop D. Jordan, *White Over Black: American Attitudes Toward The Negro, 1550–1812* (Baltimore: Penguin Books, 1968), p. 156.

14. Jordan, p. 159.

15. George M. Frederickson, *The Black Image in the White Mind,* (New York: Harper & Row), p. 278.

16. Ibid., pp. 278–79.

17. Richard Kluger, *Simple Justice* (New York: Alfred A. Knopf, 1976), p. 306.

18. Michal R. Belknap, *Federal Law and Southern Order: Racial Violence and Constitutional Conflict in the Post-Brown South* (Athens, Ga.: U. of Georgia Press, 1987), pp. 1–25.

19. William Montague Cobb, "Physical Anthropology of the American Negro," *American Journal of Physical Anthropology,* 29, June 1942, 113–23.

20. Thomas Waring, C. P. Liter, Frederick Sullens, et al., "Interviews With Southern Editors," *U.S. News & World Report,* February 24, 1956, pp. 134, 135, 138.

21. U.S. Dept of Commerce, *Statistical Abstract of the United States, 1982–1983* (Washington: GPO, 1984), p. 195.

22. *Dallas Times Herald,* August 19, 1990, p. 20.

23. Nicholas Riccardi and Leslie Berger, "Justice System Missed Chance to Jail Alleged Serial Killer," *Los Angeles Times,* November 15, 1995, p. 3; Kim Murphy, "Death in a Safe Place," *Los Angeles Times,* December 20, 1995, p. E1; *Los Angeles Times,* November 28, 1995, p. B3; November 14, 1995, p. 1.

24. "Interview with Robert Johnson," *Jet,* September 29, 1993, p. 56.

25. *New York Times,* June 20, 1995, p. 20; *Los Angeles Times,* November 23, 1995, p. C13.

26. *St. Louis American,* February 15–21, 1996, p. 2.

27. Gerda Lerner, ed. *Black Women in White America* (New York: Pantheon Books, 1972), p. 216.

28. William Oliver, "Sexual Conquests and Patterns of Black-on-Black Violence: A Structural-Cultural Perspective," *Violence and Victims* 4, 1989, 257–73.

29. John Hope Franklin, *From Slavery to Freedom* (New York: Random House, 1969), pp. 573–622.

30. Audrey Edwards, "Survey Report," *Black Enterprise,* August 1990, p. 95.

31. Black Scholar, ed. *Court of Appeal: The Black Community Speaks Out on the Racial and Sexual Politics of Thomas vs. Hill* (New York: Ballantine Books, 1992); "National Survey of Black Americans, 1979–1980," in Andrew Billingsley, *Climbing Jacob's Ladder: The Enduring Legacy of African-American Families* (New York: Simon & Schuster, 1992), p. 225.

6. Ain't I a Nigger, Too?

1. *Los Angeles Times,* November 9, 1995, p. 41.

2. Winthrop D. Jordan, *White Over Black: American Attitudes Toward the Negro, 1550–1812* (Baltimore: Penguin Books, 1968).

3. *Othello,* Act V, Scene II.
4. Jordan, p. 70.
5. Gilbert Osofsky, *The Burden of Race* (New York: Harper & Row, 1967), p. 78.
6. Mark Twain, *The Adventures of Huckleberry Finn,* Chapter 19.
7. Gene Marine, "I've Got Nothing Against the Colored, Understand," in Barry N. Schwartz and Robert Disch, eds., *White Racism,* (New York: Dell Publishing, 1970) p. 227; David Garrow, *Bearing the Cross* (New York: William Morrow, 1986), pp. 475–525.
8. Edward K. Weaver, "Racial Sensitivity Among Negro Children," in *White Racism,* pp. 184–85.
9. Rayford Logan, "The Negro as Portrayed in Representative Northern Magazines and Newspapers," in *White Racism*, pp. 395–98.
10. W. E. B. Du Bois, "That Capital 'N,' " *Crisis* 11, February 1916, 184; Robert L. Zangrando, *The NAACP and the Anti-Lynching Crusade, 1909–1950* (Philadelphia: Temple University 1980), pp. 6–7.
11. Weaver, p. 183.
12. *Los Angeles Times,* August 6, 1993, p. 1; Miles Corwin, "A Jail Without Walls," *Los Angeles Times,* October 13, 1993, p. B1.
13. *Los Angeles Times,* October 28, 1995, p. B8.
14. Richard Wright, *Uncle Tom's Children* (New York: Harper & Row, 1965), pp. 9–10.
15. Richard Pryor, *Pryor Connections* (New York: Random House, 1995), pp. 175–77.

7. The Way Things Ought Not to Be, Rush

1. Al Franken, *Rush Limbaugh Is a Big Fat Idiot* (New York: Delacorte, 1996).
2. Rush Limbaugh, *The Way Things Ought to Be* (New York: Simon & Schuster, 1992), p. 325.
3. Claudette E. Bennett, "The Black Population in the United

States, March 1989 and 1990," *Department of Commerce, U.S. Census* (Washington, D.C.: GPO, 1991), p. 7.

4. Carl Ginsberg, *Race and Media: The Enduring Life of the Moynihan Report* (New York: Institute for Media Analysis, 1989).

5. Andrew Billingsley, "Understanding African-American Family Diversity," in *State of Black America, 1990* (New York: Urban League, 1990), p. 101.

6. James Risen, "History May Judge Reaganomics Very Harshly," *Los Angeles Times,* November 8, 1992, p. D1.

7. Department of Commerce, *America's Black Population 1970–1982* (Washington, D.C.: GPO, 1984), pp. 16–17; Doris R. Entwisle and Karl L. Alexander, "Summer Setback: Race, Poverty, School Composition and Mathematics Achievements in the First Two Years of School," *American Sociological Review* 57 February 1992, 72–84.

8. Marilyn French, *The War Against Women* (New York: Summit Books, 1992), p. 185.

9. Bruce A. Chadwick and Tim B. Heaton, *Statistical Handbook on the American Family* (New York: Onyx Press, 1992). 10. David Halberstam, *The Fifties* (New York: Villard Books, 1993), pp. 508–20.

11. Limbaugh, pp. 431, 434.

12. Kim Murphy, "Not Quite Ozzie and Harriet," *Los Angeles Times,* December 19, 1995, p. 1.

13. Andrew Billingsley, *Climbing Jacob's Ladder; The Enduring Legacy of African-American Families* (New York: Simon & Schuster, 1992), p. 207.

8. Minister Farrakhan or Adolf Farrakhan?

1. *Los Angeles Times,* September 11, 1985, p. B1; September 12, 1985, p. B1; September 16, 1985, p. B5.

2. *Los Angeles Times,* October 10, 1993, p. B3.

3. *New York Times,* January 25, 1994, p. 12; *Washington Post,* February 4, 1994, p. 13.

4. Robert Scheer, "Democrats Set the Stage for Buchanan Bile," *Los Angeles Times,* February 20, 1996, p. B7.
5. Sylvester Monroe, "The Mirage of Farrakhan," *Time,* October 30, 1995, p. 52.
6. *Los Angeles Times,* October 18, 1995, p. 22
7. *Newsweek,* October 30, 1995, p. 33; *Final Call,* November 22, 1995, p. 5.
8. Marc Lacey and Sam Fulwood III, "Blacks Hear the Farrakhan Behind the Extremist Words," *Los Angeles Times,* October 22, 1995, p. 1.
9. *Los Angeles Times,* February 15, 1996, p. 4.
10. *Palm Beach Gazette,* February 1, 1996, p. 2B.

9. Why Are They Waiting to Exhale?

1. Terry McMillan, *Waiting to Exhale* (New York: Pocket Books, 1992), p. 329.
2. Sharazad Ali, *The Blackman's Guide to Understanding the Blackwoman* (Philadelphia: Civilized Press, 1989).
3. Michele Wallace, *Black Macho and the Myth of the Superwoman* (New York: Dial Press, 1978).
4. Ntozake Shange, *For Colored Girls Who Have Considered Suicide/When the Rainbow Is Enuf* (New York: Collier Books, 1977).
5. Gloria Naylor, *The Women of Brewster Place* (New York: Viking Press, 1982).
6. Alice Walker, *The Color Purple* (New York: Pocket Books, 1982).
7. Pearl Cleage, *Deals with the Devil and Other Reasons to Riot* (New York: Ballantine Books, 1993), p. 153.
8. Bell Hooks, *Ain't I a Woman* (Boston: South End Press, 1981), pp. 88–90, 94.
9. Frederick Engels, *The Origin of the Family, Private Property and the State* (Moscow: Foreign Languages Publishing House, 1960), pp. 120–36.
10. Eugene Hillman, *Polygamy Reconsidered: African Plural*

Marriage (Maryknoll, N.Y.: Orbis Books, 1975), pp. 43–44.

11. Andrew Billingsley, *Black Families in White America* (Englewood Cliffs, N.J.: Prentice-Hall, 1968), pp. 38–48, 94–95, 240–43; Herbert Gutman provides solid evidence that for nearly a century following emancipation there were marked differences in the domestic patterns of black and white families *(The Black Family in Slavery and Freedom, 1750–1925* [New York: Random House, 1975], pp. 363–460).

12. Bell Hooks, *Talking Back, Thinking Feminist, Thinking Black* (Boston: South End Press, 1989), p. 155.

13. Gayle Pollard, "Interview with Terry McMillan," *Los Angeles Times,* January 14, 1996, p. M3.

14. *Los Angeles Times,* December 28, 1995, p. F1.

15. Amy Tan, *The Joy Luck Club* (New York: G. P. Putnam, 1989); Isabel Allende, *Eva Luna* (Barcelona: Plaza & Janes Editores, 1991).

16. "Interview with Terry McMillan," *Los Angeles Times,* January 14, 1996, Section M, p. 3.

17. Andrew Billingsley, *Climbing Jacob's Ladder: The Enduring Legacy of African-American Families* (New York: Simon & Schuster, 1992), pp. 243, 245–61.

18. Earl Ofari Hutchinson, *Black Fatherhood: The Guide to Male Parenting* (Los Angeles: Middle Passage Press, 1992).

10. No Thriller for Michael Jackson

1. Sonia Nazario and Amy Wallace, "International Furor Stirred by Allegations on Jackson," *Los Angeles Times,* August 26, 1993, p. 1.

2. "Sexual Predators: Can They Be Stopped?" *U.S. News & World Report,* September 19, 1994, pp. 65–76.

3. Quoted in *Nation,* October 11, 1993, p. 376.

4. *New York Times,* December 7, 1995, p. B16.

5. *Los Angeles Times,* January 26, 1996, p. F1.

6. Robert Joseph Taylor, Linda M. Chatters, M. Belinda Tucker,

and Edith Lewis, "Developments in Research on Black Families," *Journal of Marriage and the Family* 52, November 1990, 993–1014.

11. What's Love Got to Do with It? More Than You Think

1. Tina Turner, *I, Tina* (New York: William Morrow, 1986), pp. 206–207.
2. Audrey Edwards, "What Becomes a Sex Goddess Most," *Essence,* July 1993, p. 52.
3. Turner, p. 154.
4. Leonard Berkowitz, "The Study of Urban Violence," *American Behavioral Scientist* 11, March-April 1968, 14–17.

12. The War on Drugs *Is* a War on Black Males

1. Ron Harris, "Blacks Feel Brunt of Drug War," *Los Angeles Times,* April 22, 1990, p. 1.
2. Sam Vincent, "Is the Drug War Racist?," *USA Today,* July 23–25, 1993, p. 1.
3. Margo Walker, "Black Students Just Say No," *Emerge,* August 1991, p. 4.
4. *Los Angeles Times,* February 7, 1996, p. B3.
5. Jeanette Covington, "Self-Esteem and Deviance: The Effects of Race and Gender," *Criminology* 24, November 1986, 105–38.
6. Kirk A. Johnson, "Objective News and Other Myths: The Poisoning of Young Black Minds," *Journal of Negro History* 60, 1991, 332.
7. Lionel McPherson, "News Media, Racism and the Drug War," *Extra!,* April 5, 1992, p. 5.
8. Linda S. Wong and Bruce K. Alexander, "Cocaine-Related Deaths: Media Coverage in the War on Drugs," *The Journal of Drug Issues* 21, 1991, 105–19.

9. Beny J. Primm, "Drug Use: Special Implications for Black America," in *State of Black America, 1987* (New York: Urban League, 1987), p. 147.

10. Randolph N. Stone, "The War on Drugs: The Wrong Enemy and the Wrong Battlefield," *National Bar Association Magazine,* December 1989, pp. 18–35.

11. Vincent, op. cit.

12. Jim Newton, "Judges Voice Anger Over Mandatory U.S. Sentencing," *Los Angeles Times,* August 21, 1993, p. 1; Douglas C. McDonald and Kenneth E. Carlson, *Sentencing in the Federal Courts: Does Race Matter?* (Washington, D.C.: Dept. of Justice, December 1993).

13. *Los Angeles Times,* April 22, 1990, p. 1.

14. Miles Corwin, "Heroin's New Popularity Claims Unlikely Victims," *Los Angeles Times,* February 11, 1996, p. 1.

15. Mark Whitaker, "A Crisis of Shattered Dreams," *Newsweek,* May 6, 1991, pp. 28–31.

16. Victor Merina, "Joe Morgan Suit Protests Drug Profile," *Los Angeles Times,* August 7, 1990, p. B1; *Los Angeles Times,* November 17, 1993, p. 1.

17. Steven Belenko, Jeffrey Fagan, and Ko-Lin Chin, "Criminal Justice Response to Crack," *Journal of Research in Crime and Delinquency* 28, February 1991, 55–74.

18. *Los Angeles Times,* December 15, 1995, p. 31.

13. The Other Boyz N the Hood

1. *Time,* February 26, 1996, p. 71.

2. Claudette E. Bennett, *The Black Population in the United States, March 1989 and March 1990,* (Washington, D.C.: Dept. of Commerce, Bureau of the Census, GPO, DC, August, 1991), Table B, p. 3; Sylvester Monroe, "Diversity Comes to Elite Prep Schools," *Emerge,* August 1993, pp. 50–54; *Chicago Sun Times,* August 1, 1994, p. 24.

3. Michael Hughes and David Demo, "Self-Perceptions of Black Americans: Self-Esteem and Personal Efficacy," *American Journal of Sociology* 95, July 1989, 132–59.

4. Bennet Harrison, "For Blacks a Degree Doesn't Automatically Mean Higher Incomes," *Los Angeles Times,* September 2, 1990, p. M4.

5. Sheryl Stolberg, "150,000 Are in Gangs, Report by D.A. Claims," *Los Angeles Times,* May 22, 1992, p. 1; Rosalind X. Moore, "L.A. Police Hang 'Gang Banger' Label on City's Young Black Males," *Final Call,* June 15, 1992, p. 2.

6. John A. Backstrand, Don C. Gibbons, and Joseph F. Jones, "Who Is in Jail," *Crime & Delinquency* 38, April 1992, 219–229; Jack Katz, "Gangs Aren't the Cause of Crime," *Los Angeles Times,* May 31, 1992, p. B5; Steven H. Stumpf, "Crack: Crisis in the African-American Community," *Conference Report,* April 3, 1990.

7. *Detroit Free Press,* November 12, 1994, p. 6.

8. Barbara Cottman Becnel, "Interview with Stanley (Tookie) Williams," *Los Angeles Times,* August 22, 1993, Section M, p. 3.

9. Kenneth Clark & Mamie Clark, *Racial Identification and Preferences in Negro Children* (New York: Holt, 1947).

10. Darlene Powell Hopson and Derek S. Hopson, "Implications of Doll Color Preferences Among Black Preschool Children and White Preschool Children," *Journal of Black Psychology,* 14, February 1988, 57–63; Michael McMillan, "The Doll Test Studies: From Cabbage Patch to Self-Concept," *Journal of Black Psychology* 14, February 1988, 69–72; Kathryn P. Johnsen and Morris L. Medley, "Academic Self-Concept Among Black High School Seniors: An Examination of Perceived Agreement with Selected Others," *Phylon,* 39, 1978, 264–74.

11. Andrea Ford and Carla Rivera, "Hope Takes Hold as Bloods, Crips Say Truce Is for Real," *Los Angeles Times,* May 21, 1992, p. 1.

12. Jill Smolowe, "Danger in the Safety Zone," *Time,* August 23, 1993, p. 29; J. Michael Kennedy, "Students Armed and Dangerous," *Los Angeles Times,* October 10, 1991, p. 1.

13. *National Television Violence Study* (Studio City, Ca.: Mediascope, Inc., 1994–95); Carolyn A. Stroman, "Television's

Role in the Socialization of African-American Children and Adolescents," *Journal of Negro History* 60, 1991, 315–18.

14. Marvin Wolfgang and Franco Ferracuti, *The Subculture of Violence* (London: Tavistock Publications, 1967); Robert Nash Parker, "Poverty, Subculture of Violence and Type of Homicide," *Social Forces* 19, December 1989, 980–1007.

15. Ron Harris, "Hand of Punishment Weighs Heavily on Black Youth," *Los Angeles Times,* August 24, 1993, p. 1.

16. *Los Angeles Times,* December 21, 1993, p. 1.

17. Ronald L. Simons and Phyllis A. Gray, "Perceived Blocked Opportunity as an Explanation of Delinquency Among Lower-Class Black Males: A Research Note," *Journal of Research in Crime and Delinquency* 26, February 1989, 90–101.

18. Jesse Katz, "Summit of Gangs Takes Aim at Peace," *Los Angeles Times,* May 2, 1993, p. 1.

14. Ghetto Chic

1. *Los Angeles Bay Observer,* February 10, 1996, p. 4; *Los Angeles Times,* October 25, 1995, p. F1.

2. "White's Myths About Blacks," *U.S. News & World Report,* November 19, 1992, pp. 45–47.

15. Colin Powell: An American Journey or American Dilemma?

1. Mark E. Neely, Jr. *The Last Best Hope of Earth* (Cambridge, Mass.: Harvard U. Press, 1993), p. 157.

2. *Los Angeles Times,* October 7, 1995, p. 1.

3. *Los Angeles Times,* October 17, 1995, p. 11.

4. Evan Thomas, "Why He Got Out," *Newsweek,* November 20, 1995, p. 42.

5. Colin Powell, *My American Journey* (New York: Random House, 1995), p. 401.

6. Ibid.
7. Powell, p. 402; Robert Parry & Norman Soloman, "Powell Media Mania," *Extra!,* January-February 1996, p. 17.
8. *Los Angeles Times,* October 30, 1995, p. 17; October 26, 1995, p. 1.
9. *Los Angeles Times,* November 2, 1995, p. 18.
10. *Los Angeles Times,* November 16, 1995, p. 5.

16. The Never-Ending Saga of O. J. Simpson

1. *Sports Illustrated,* June 27, 1994, p. 20.
2. *Newsweek,* August 29, 1994, p. 44.
3. *Daily Trojan,* January 1, 1968, p. 12.
4. Dick Belsky, *The Juice* (New York: McKay, 1977) p. 27.
5. *Time,* June 27, 1994, p. 20.
6. *Time,* July 1, 1994, pp. 20–21.
7. *Wall Street Journal,* March 22, 1995, p. 1; *Los Angeles Times,* October 7, 1995, p. 1; January 28, 1996, p. 1; July 1, 1995, p. 30.
8. *L.A. Sentinel,* August 4, 1994, p. 1.
9. *Newsweek,* August 22, 1994, p. 42.
10. *New York Times,* December 29, 1991, p. 4.
11. *Los Angeles Times,* June 4, 1995, p. M3.
12. O. J. Simpson, *I Want to Tell You* (Boston: Little, Brown, 1995).
13. *Los Angeles Times,* September 9, 1994, p. 3.
14. Simpson, p. 122.
15. *Los Angeles Times,* February 21, 1996, p. B1.
16. *Los Angeles Times,* October 5, 1995, p. 6; October 12, 1995, p. B9; October 30, 1995, p. 19.
17. *Los Angeles Times,* October 4, 1995, p. 11.
18. *Los Angeles Times,* January 26, 1996, p. F1.
19. *Time,* January 22, 1996, p. 34; February 5, 1996, p. F2.

America's Hidden Agenda Against Black Males: A Postscript

1. "New Report Reveals Young Whites Are More Biased Against Blacks Than Older Whites Are," *Jet,* July 5, 1993, pp. 26–29.
2. Joe R. Feagin, "The Continuing Significance of Race: Anti-Black Discrimination in Public Places," *American Sociological Review* 56, 1991, 101–16.
3. Bob Baker, "Stereotypes That Won't Go Away," *Los Angeles Times,* May 31, 1992, p. 1.
4. "Crime: A Conspiracy of Silence," *Newsweek,* May 18, 1992, p. 37; Marc Mauer, "Americans Behind Bars," *Criminal Justice* 6, Winter 1992, 12–18.

Bibliography

Anderson, David C. *Crime and the Politics of Hysteria: How the Willie Horton Story Changed American Justice*. New York: Times Books, 1995.

Ashe, Arthur, Jr. *A Hard Road to Glory: A History of the Black Athlete, 1619–1918, Vol. 1*. New York: World Books, 1988.

Bagdikian, Ben. *The Media Monopoly*. Boston: Beacon Press, 1990.

Bardolph, Richard, ed. *The Civil Rights Record: Black America and the Law, 1849–1970*. New York: Thomas Y. Crowell, Co., 1970.

Billingsley, Andrew. *Climbing Jacob's Ladder: The Enduring Legacy of African-American Families*. New York: Simon & Schuster, 1992.

Black Scholar, ed. *Court of Appeal: The Black Community Speaks Out on the Racial and Sexual Politics of Thomas vs. Hill*. New York: Ballantine Books, 1992.

Boggle, Donald. *Toms, Coons, Mulattos, Mammies and Bucks*. New York: Continuum Publishing Co., 1989.

Clark, Kenneth and Mamie Clark. *Racial Identification and Preferences in Negro Children*. New York: Holt, 1947.

Edwards, Harry. *The Revolt of the Black Athlete.* New York: The Free Press, 1970.

Franklin, John Hope. *From Slavery to Freedom.* New York: Random House, 1969.

Frederickson, George M. *The Black Image in the White Mind, 1817–1914.* New York: Harper & Row, 1971.

French, Marilyn. *The War Against Women.* New York: Summit Books, 1992.

Ginsberg, Carl. *Race and Media: The Enduring Life of the Moynihan Report.* New York: Institute for Media Analysis, 1989.

Gross, Seymour L. and John Edward Hardy. *Image of the Negro in American Literature.* Chicago: University of Chicago Press, 1966.

Halberstam, David. *The Powers That Be.* New York: Alfred A. Knopf, 1979.

Hooks, Bell. *Talking Back: Thinking Feminist, Thinking Black.* Boston: South End Press, 1989.

Hutchinson, Earl Ofari. *Black Fatherhood: The Guide to Male Parenting.* Los Angeles: Middle Passage Press, 1992.

Jordan, Winthrop D. *White Over Black: American Attitudes Toward the Negro, 1550–1812.* Baltimore: Penguin, 1968.

Kluger, Richard. *Simple Justice.* New York: Alfred A. Knopf, 1976.

Lerner, Gerda, ed. *Black Women in White America.* New York: Pantheon Books, 1972.

Limbaugh, Rush. *The Way Things Ought to Be.* New York: Pocket Books, 1992.

McMillan, Terry. *Waiting to Exhale* New York: Pocket Books, 1992.

O'Reilly, Kenneth. *Nixon's Piano: Presidents and Racial Politics from Washington to Clinton.* New York: The Free Press, 1995.

Powell, Colin. *My American Journey.* New York: Random House, 1995.

Schwartz, Barry N. and Robert Disch. *White Racism.* New York: Dell Publishing, 1970.

Sharkey, Joe. *Deadly Greed: The Stuart Murder Case in Boston and the 1980s.* New York: Prentice Hall Press, 1991.

Simpson, O. J. *I Want to Tell You.* Boston: Little, Brown, 1995.

State of Black America, 1987. New York: Urban League, 1987.

State of Black America, 1990. New York: Urban League, 1990.

State of Black America, 1993. New York: Urban League, 1993.

State of Black America, 1994. New York: Urban League, 1994.

Wolfgang, Marvin and Franco Ferracuti. *The Subculture of Violence.* London: Tavistock Publications, 1967.

Wood, Forrest G. *The Black Scare: The Racist Response to Emancipation and Reconstruction.* Berkeley: University of California Press, 1968.

Zangrando, Robert L. *The NAACP Crusade Against Lynching, 1909–1950.* Philadelphia: Temple University Press, 1980.

Index